THE CELTIC WAY OF EVANGELISM

THE CELTIC WAY OF EVANGELISM

HOW CHRISTIANITY CAN
REACH THE WEST... AGAIN

GEORGE G. HUNTER III

ABINGDON PRESS
Nashville

THE CELTIC WAY OF EVANGELISM
HOW CHRISTIANITY CAN REACH THE WEST ... AGAIN

This book is printed on recycled, acid-free, elemental-chlorine–free paper.

Book design by J. S. Laughbaum

Library of Congress Cataloging-in-Publication Data

Hunter, George G.
    The Celtic way of evangelism : how Christianity can reach the West again / George G. Hunter III.
        p.   c m.
    Includes bibliographical references and index.
    ISBN 0-687-08585-3 (alk. paper)
    1. Celtic Church.   2. Missions.   I. Title.

BR748.H86 2000
270'.089'916—dc21   99-048173

The poem on page 72 is taken from *The Celtic Churches: A History A.D. 200 to 1200* by John T. McNeill, copyright © 1974 by The University of Chicago Press. All rights reserved. Used by permission of The University of Chicago Press.

Selections from *How the Irish Saved Civilization: The Untold Story of Ireland's Heroic Role from the Fall of Rome to the Rise of Medieval Europe*, by Thomas Cahill, are copyright © 1995 by Thomas Cahill. Used by permission of Doubleday, a division of Random House, Inc.

The poem on page 35, "Exams," is from *Celtic Prayers for Everyday Life: Prayers for Every Occasion*, by Ray Simpson. Copyright © 1998 by Ray Simpson. All rights reserved. Reproduced by permission of Hodder and Stoughton Limited.

We acknowledge the Four Courts Press, Dublin, Ireland, for kind permission to quote from *St. Patrick's World* by Liam de Paor.

Passages from Bede's *Ecclesiastical History of the English People*, edited by Judith McClure and Roger Collins, 1994 edition, are used by permission of Oxford University Press.

00 01 02 03 04 05 06 07 08 09—10 9 8 7 6 5 4 3

MANUFACTURED IN THE UNITED STATES OF AMERICA

To Ted Runyon,

Professor of Theology Emeritus,
Candler School of Theology, Emory University

—*whose course in Theology of the Church and*
Sacraments, a third of a century ago, inspired
the understanding and the wider appreciation
behind this project.

CONTENTS

PREFACE

he Church, in the Western world, faces populations who are increasingly "secular"—people with no Christian memory, who don't know what we Christians are talking about. These populations are increasingly "urban"—and out of touch with God's "natural revelation." These populations are increasingly "postmodern"; they have graduated from Enlightenment ideology and are more peer driven, feeling driven, and "right-brained" than their forebears. These populations are increasingly "neo-barbarian"; they lack "refinement" or "class," and their lives are often out of control. These populations are increasingly receptive—exploring worldview options from Astrology to Zen—and are often looking "in all the wrong places" to make sense of their lives and find their soul's true home.

In the face of this changing Western culture, many Western Church leaders are in denial; they plan and do church as though next year will be 1957. Furthermore, most of the Western Church leaders who are not in denial do not know how to engage the epidemic numbers of secular, postmodern, neo-barbarians outside (and inside) their churches. Moreover, most of the few who do know what to do are intuitive geniuses who cannot teach others what they know (or charismatic leaders who cannot yet be cloned). The mainline Western Churches, Roman Catholic and Protestant, lack both the precedent and the "paradigm" for engaging the West's emerging mission fields. There is, however, a model upon which Western Christians can draw as they face this daunting new situation. The ancient movement known as Celtic Christianity can show us some ways forward in the twenty-first century.

Most Western Church leaders would never guess that ancient Celtic Christianity could show the way today for two reasons. First, they assume that no expression of ancient Christianity could be relevant to the challenges we now face. Second, they assume that the only useful stream of insight is, by definition, confined to Roman Christianity and its Reformation offshoots. Few of us study other branches of the Church—such as the Eastern Orthodox churches, or the Oriental Orthodox churches (Armenian, Coptic, etc.), or the Slavic churches, or the Waldensian churches, or the Thomas churches of India, or the African Independent churches, or other Third World churches, or the world's Pentecostal churches. The typical "Church History" course barely mentions them.

The whole of Church History does represent, of course, an intimidating range of culturally specific church histories, and a class has only so much lecture time and reading time. Nevertheless, the assumption is blatant: the only church history really worth knowing is Latin church history and its Reformation spin-offs. When a colleague heard I was writing a book on how the ancient Celtic Christians did ministry and mission, he asked, "What could we possibly learn from them?" When I lead field seminars on the subject, a few people who are "into" Celtic music, art, poetry, dance, or spirituality bring interest to the subject, as well as those who are interested in recovering their Irish or Scottish roots. Most people, however, bring low expectations, wondering why Hunter would bore people with his new antiquarian obsession!

Two books were published in the 1990s, however, that

put the topic on the "map" and stimulated new interest in Celtic Christianity. Thomas Cahill's *How the Irish Saved Civilization* tells the story, with great flair, of the Celtic movement's evangelization of Ireland, and Scotland, as well as much of England and Europe. John Finney's *Recovering the Past* sketches the basic way that the Celtic Christian movement approached mission vis-à-vis the Roman way. This project stands on the shoulders of Cahill and Finney.

Two other recent sources were immensely useful to this project. Liam de Poar's *Saint Patrick's World* puts in one volume, in English translation, the ancient Gaelic and Latin sources that tell us much of what is knowable about St. Patrick and his mission to the Irish Celts. The Oxford University Press edition of Bede's *Ecclesiastical History of the English People*, with many endnotes, makes this classic history of the post–Irish expansion of Celtic Christianity even more useful than before.

De Poar and Bede were indispensable because I approached this topic as a communication theorist and missiologist, with no credentials and glaring deficiencies for interpreting ancient and medieval history. My Latin and Greek are beyond rusty. I have no knowledge of Gaelic, nor any other Celtic language, nor any of the languages employed as Celtic Christians reached the "barbarian" peoples of Europe.

Some critics may charge that I have reached some conclusions on insufficient evidence. If, however, we know that all (or most) effective advocates do certain things, or that all (or most) Christian movements do certain things, or that all (or most) primal peoples respond to the gospel in certain ways, we can venture related conclusions about Celtic Christianity with less evidence than if Celtic Christian sources were our only sources of strategic Christian insight.

I have already presented some of this material to the 1997 meeting of the Academy for Evangelism (and its journal); the 1998 meeting of the American Society for Church Growth (and its journal); and, in 1999, in lectureships at the United Methodist Congress on Evangelism in New Orleans, North Park Theological Seminary, Hiwassee College, and Cliff College in England; as well as in classes and forums at Asbury Theological Seminary.

I am grateful to Asbury for sabbatical time for research and writing; to Dr. Howard Snyder (a *real* historian) and Dr. Ella Hunter (a candid wife!), who read the manuscript and offered invaluable suggestions; to library personnel at Trinity College, Dublin, the Iona Community, the Divinity School of Aberdeen University, and Marygate House, Holy Island for welcoming and helping an academic interloper from "the colonies"; and to Carol Childress and her colleagues at Leadership Network whose grant made possible the library research and several site visits. The days spent in "solitary" at the site of St. Patrick's first church (Saul), at his grave (at Downpatrick), and at the ancient sites of Glendalough, Iona, and Lindisfarne enabled my soul to sense the vision that once drove "apostolic teams" of men and women to abandon almost everything they cherished for the sake of lost people who needed to be found.

This book is presented with the naive confidence that, if Western Church leaders are willing to love the Lord of the Harvest with their minds as well as their hearts, and are willing to learn from a once-great movement outside of the Roman paradigm, then Christianity can become contagious once more across North America and Europe in the twenty-first century.

Chapter 1

The Gospel to the Irish

n the late fourth century (or early fifth century) A.D., Patrick was growing up in (what is now) northeast England. His people were "Britons," one of the "Celtic" peoples then populating the British Isles, though Patrick's aristocratic family had gone "Roman" during the Roman occupation of England. So Patrick was more culturally Roman than Celtic; his first language was Latin, though he understood some of the "Welsh" spoken by the lower classes. His family was Christian; his grandfather was a priest. Patrick had acquired some Christian teaching, and he undoubtedly knew the catechism, but he became only a nominal Christian; he ridiculed the clergy and, in the company of other "alienated" and "ungoverned" youth, he lived toward the wild side.[1]

When Patrick was sixteen, a band of Celtic pirates from Ireland invaded the region; they captured Patrick and many other young men, forced them onto a ship, sailed to Ireland, and sold them into slavery. The pirates sold Patrick to a prosperous tribal chief and druid named Miliuc (Miliuc moccu Boin), who put Patrick to work herding cattle.

During his years of enslavement, Patrick experienced three profound changes. First, the periods when Patrick was isolated in the wilderness herding cattle connected him with what theologians call the "natural revelation" of

God. He sensed with the winds, the seasons, the creatures, and the nights under the stars the presence of God; he identified this presence with the Triune God he had learned about in the catechism. In his (more or less) autobiographical "Declaration" Patrick tells us

> After I had arrived in Ireland, I found myself pasturing flocks daily, and I prayed a number of times each day. More and more the love and fear of God came to me, and faith grew and my spirit was exercised, until I was praying up to a hundred times every day and in the night nearly as often.[2]

Patrick became a devout Christian, and the change was obvious to his captors.

Second, Patrick changed in another way during the periods he spent with his captors in their settlement. He came to understand the Irish Celtic people, and their language and culture, with the kind of intuitive profundity that is usually possible only, as in Patrick's case, from the "underside."

Third, Patrick came to love his captors, to identify with them, and to hope for their reconciliation to God. One day, he would feel they were his people.

One night, after six years of captivity, a voice spoke to Patrick in a dream, saying, "You are going home. Look! Your ship is ready!" The voice directed him to flee for his freedom the next morning. He awakened before daybreak, walked to a seacoast, saw the ship, and negotiated his way on board.

The data for piecing together the next quarter century of Patrick's story are limited, and scholars disagree when interpreting the scant data we have, but the story line runs something like this. The ship probably took Patrick to Gaul, though perhaps to England. He may have spent considerable time in Gaul (perhaps with the monastic community of St. Martin of Tours), and he may have gone to Rome, but he eventually returned to his people in England. He trained for the priesthood perhaps in Rome, or in Gaul, more likely in England. His training immersed his mind in the scriptures, and grounded him in the basic orthodox theology that prevailed in the Western Church of that time. He then served for years as a faithful parish priest in England.

One night, at the age of forty-eight—already past a man's life expectancy in the fifth century—Patrick experienced another dream that was to change his life again. An angel named Victor approached him with letters from his former captors in Ireland. As he read one of the letters, he "imagined in that moment that [he] heard the voice of those very people who were near the wood of Foclut, . . . and they cried out, as with one voice 'We appeal to you, holy servant boy, to come and walk among us.' "[3]

When Patrick awakened the next morning, he interpreted the dream as his "Macedonian Call" to take Christianity's gospel to the Celtic peoples of Ireland. He proposed, to his ecclesiastical superiors, that he be sent on this mission. The bishops of the British Church, probably with the strong encouragement of Pope Celestine, affirmed Patrick's vision. Patrick was ordained a bishop, and appointed to Ireland, as history's first missionary bishop. The tradition tells us that he arrived in Ireland, with a modest entourage of priests, seminarians, and others, in A.D. 432.[4]

Patrick's mission to Ireland was to be such an unprecedented undertaking that it is impossible to understate its magnitude and significance. Why? Because the Irish Celtic peoples were "barbarians."

The oldest and most perennial "issue" in the history of Christianity's world mission hangs upon two terms: "Christianizing" and "Civilizing." In a classic essay, Pierce Beaver tells us that mission leaders, including the

Protestant mission leaders of the last several hundred years, have usually assumed that the two goals of a Christian mission are to "evangelize" a people and to "civilize" them. Beaver explains that, in the formative period of Protestant mission, there was never even

> debate about the legitimacy of the stress on the civilizing function of missions. Debate was only about priority; which came first, christianization or civilization? Some held that a certain degree of civilization was first necessary to enable a people to understand and accept the faith. Others argued that one should begin with christianization since the gospel inevitably produced a hunger for civilization. Most persons believed that the two mutually interacted and should be stressed equally and simultaneously.[5]

In practice, a Protestant mission's "civilizing" objectives for a people were scripted by the specific customs of the sending nation. Beaver reports, for instance, that in the sixteenth- to eighteenth-century period of Spain's colonial expansion, "Spain . . . endeavored to transplant Christianity and civilization both according to the Spanish model."[6] Likewise, the seventeenth century Puritan mission to Native American Indians organized converts into churches and into "Christian towns" in order to enculturate the Indians into what Cotton Mather called "a more decent and English way of living."[7] Beaver reports that

> even in countries with a high culture, such as India and China, European missionaries stressed the "civilizing" objective as much as their brethren in primitive regions because they regarded the local culture as degenerate and superstitious—a barrier to christianization.[8]

The much earlier period of Roman Christianity's expansion, prior to Patrick, had struggled with these same issues but was afflicted by two versions of this problem both different from the later, Protestant versions. The perspective of the ancient Roman Christian leaders can be baldly stated in two sentences: (1) Roman Christian leaders assumed that a population had to be civilized "enough" already to be Christianized, that is, that some degree of civilization was a prerequisite to Christianization. (2) Once a sufficiently civilized population became Christian, they were expected in time to read and speak Latin, to adopt other Roman customs, and to do church "the Roman way."

This Roman perspective seems to have surfaced in the second century and then prevailed until the time of Patrick. The first century apostolic movement reached several peoples, at least, who were neither "civilized" nor subsequently "Romanized." The apostolic tradition reports, for instance, that Andrew planted Christianity among barbarian populations of Scythia, that Thomas reached Parthians and Syrians, and that Matthew's martyrdom ignited a Christian movement in a cannibal population in Anthropophagi.[9]

From the second century, however, historians report no organized missions to the "barbarian" peoples, such as the Celts, the Goths, the Visigoths, the Vandals, the Franks, the Frisians, the Huns, and the Vikings, who lived at the fringes of the Roman Empire.[10] By now, the Church assumed that reaching barbarians was impossible; a population, by definition, had to be literate and rational enough to understand Christianity, and cultured and civil enough to become real Christians if they *did* understand it.

Why did the Roman Church regard the Irish Celts as "barbarians?" What could have given them that idea? The Romans did not know the Irish people. Ireland was geographically isolated from the Roman Empire; Rome had never conquered or controlled Ireland, or even placed a Roman colony there.

Historically, however, Rome had observed Celtic peoples. The history of the *Keltoi* peoples predated the Roman Empire by more than a thousand years. Celtic tribes had once been the dominant population of Europe, and they had been the greatest warriors of Europe. The European Celts were not a race, with a common genetic lineage, so much as a "macroculture," or a cultural and linguistic family of peoples. However, each tribe was distinct from the others, with its own gods, laws, customs, and language or dialect.[11]

Consequently, the Celtic tribes had little experience in organizing across tribal lines. So, in warfare, each Celtic tribe fought for itself, but was not organized to fight in league with other tribes against a common enemy. An analogy should clarify this important point. A zoologist once informed me that a tiger will defeat a lion in battle; but five lions will defeat five tigers because the lions fight together and the tigers do not, so the five lions take on one tiger at a time. Each Celtic tribe was a formidable tiger in battle, greatly respected and feared. The Romans, with legendary strength in organization and coordination, were the lions in a lengthy series of battles against specific tribes to incrementally expand their empire.

For two centuries, the lions pushed the tigers westward to "the Celtic fringe" of western Europe—like Gaul, Brittany, and the British Isles. In Patrick's time, the British Isles featured several Celtic peoples—most notably the Britons in (what is now) England, the Picts in (what is now) Scotland, and the Irish (or the Scots) in Ireland. In the two centuries following Patrick, hoards of the Irish invaded Scotland and absorbed the Picts, thus accounting for the term "Scots-Irish" and explaining the similarities in Scottish and Irish accents and culture to this day.

So the Romans had observed some Celtic peoples historically; indeed, Julius Caesar had even written about them. Furthermore, the Romans had heard many rumors about the Irish Celts. Why did the Romans think of the Celtic peoples, particularly the Irish, as "barbarians"? Well, the Romans tended to regard everyone who wasn't culturally Roman as "barbarian"![12] The Romans regarded literacy as a sure and certain sign of being civilized; the Irish Celts did not read and write and were not interested. The Irish were "emotional" people, volatile personalities known for letting the full range of human emotions get out of control. The Romans virtually equated "being civilized" with emotional control. In warfare "all the Celts . . . stripped before battle and rushed their enemy naked, carrying sword and shield but wearing only sandals and torc—a twisted, golden neck ornament . . . [while] howling and, it seemed, possessed by demons!"[13] (Roman soldiers would have noticed that!) Furthermore, the Celts were known to decapitate some conquered enemy warriors,[14] and to practice human sacrifice in some of their religious rituals.[15] For reasons such as these, the Romans stereotyped the Irish Celts as "barbarians," and therefore probably unreachable.[16] Nevertheless, by Patrick's time there was some interest, especially at the papal level, in the possibility of reaching "barbarians," and that is probably why Patrick's Macedonian vision found support.

Patrick's mission to Ireland was unprecedented and widely assumed to be impossible. The Irish context of that period, however, provided some strategic advantages for Patrick's mission. Ireland was populated by about 150 *tuaths*—extended tribes—each tribe fiercely loyal to its tribal king.[17] Ireland's total population numbered between 200,000 and 500,000 people.[18] By Patrick's time, all of the tribes spoke the same language that Patrick had learned while a slave, and they now shared more or less the same culture, so Patrick understood them.

Indeed, the fact that Patrick understood the people and their language, their issues, and their ways, serves as the most strategically significant single insight that was to drive the wider expansion of Celtic Christianity, and stands as perhaps our greatest single learning from this movement. There is no shortcut to understanding the people. When you understand the people, you will often know what to say and do, and how. When the people know that the Christians understand them, they infer that maybe the High God understands them too.

Brendan Lehane identifies other contextual factors conducive to a Christian movement in fifth-century Ireland.[19] For, perhaps, one thousand years, no outside religion had penetrated Ireland; so, without a tradition of suspicion, the Irish gave Christian advocates a willing hearing. Philosophically, the Irish were accustomed to paradox, which prepared them to appreciate some of Christianity's central truth claims. Their belief that Ultimate Reality is complex, and their fascination with rhetorical triads and the number three opened them to Christianity's Triune God. Christianity's contrasting features of idealism and practicality engaged identical traits in the Irish character. No other religion could have engaged the Irish people's love for heroism, stories, and legends like Christianity. Some of Christianity's values and virtues essentially matched, or fulfilled, ideals in Irish piety and folklore. Irish Christianity was able to deeply affirm, and fulfill, the Irish love for nature and their belief in the closeness of the divine. Christianity fueled and amplified the Irish love for learning and adapted to the Irish preference for oral tradition and memorizing rather than writing and reading. Christianity's strategic approach contrasted, however, with what the Irish had observed in their primal religion. The Druids, Ireland's traditional religious leaders for centuries, had enhanced their status and power through closely guarding their secret knowledge. The people easily perceived the difference in Christianity, which was "open to all, it kept no secrets from anyone, and had as its aim the happiness of the whole population."[20]

Patrick, after years of reflection on how the Irish might be reached, now moved into mission. We do not know nearly all we would like to know about his movement's mission approach and methods, though our discussion of the Irish context included several answers. Often, his writings tantalize us more than they inform us. Moreover, we cannot be certain how much of the Celtic Christian movement's later approach in Ireland, Scotland, England, and Europe was pioneered and modeled by Patrick, and how much the approach was developed after him. But, from a handful of ancient sources,[21] we can piece together the following outline of a typical approach, which undoubtedly varied from one time and setting to another.

Patrick's entourage would have included a dozen or so people, including priests, seminarians, and two or three women.[22] Upon arrival at a tribal settlement, Patrick would engage the king and other opinion leaders, hoping for their conversion,[23] or at least their clearance, to camp near the people and form into a community of faith adjacent to the tribal settlement. The "apostolic" (in the sense of the Greek word meaning "sent on mission") team would meet the people, engage them in conversation and in ministry, and look for people who appeared receptive. They would pray for sick people, and for possessed people, and they would counsel people and mediate conflicts. On at least one occasion, Patrick blessed a river and prayed for the people to catch more fish. They would engage in some open-air speaking, probably employing parable, story, poetry, song, visual symbols, visual arts and, perhaps, drama to engage the Celtic people's remarkable imaginations. Often, we think, Patrick would receive the people's questions and then speak to those questions collectively.[24]

The apostolic band would probably welcome responsive

people into their group fellowship to worship with them, pray with them, minister to them, converse with them, and break bread together.[25] One band member or another would probably join with each responsive person to reach out to relatives and friends. The mission team typically spent weeks, or even months, as a ministering community of faith within the tribe. The church that emerged within the tribe would have been astonishingly indigenous.

If God blessed the efforts of Patrick's band and the people responded in faith, they built a church. Indeed, the salient goal of the mission to each settlement was to plant a church, and Patrick often led in the decision regarding the chapel's location. Sometimes one or two members of the entourage would fan out and reach a nearby community. On one occasion, a young nun named Mathona "went across the Mountain . . . and founded a free church at Tamnach."[26] Sometimes they planted more than one church in the same settlement. The founding of a church would have involved a public service in which the church's first converts were baptized into the faith. When the apostolic entourage moved on, Patrick would leave one of his protégés behind to be the new church's priest, "leaving with them a textbook of elementary Christian instruction."[27] Typically, one or two of their young people, who would one day be priests or nuns, would join the entourage as it moved on to another tribal settlement, to plant another church.[28] Patrick engaged in this group approach to apostolic ministry for twenty-eight years, until his death around A.D. 460. As the movement grew, more of his time was also devoted to administration, preparing and ordaining priests and, like Paul before him, visiting the churches he had planted. By this time, however, other leaders were leading apostolic bands in missions to Celtic settlements.

What had Patrick and his people achieved in his twenty-eight-year mission to the "barbarian" Irish Celts? The question cannot be answered with mathematical precision, but estimates are possible. We believe there were some Christians, perhaps Christian slaves or traders and their families, already living in Ireland by A.D. 432, but there was no indigenous Irish Christian movement before Patrick. Patrick and his people launched a movement. They baptized "many thousands" of people, probably tens of thousands. Tirechan refers, usually by name, to at least fifty-five churches that Patrick's team planted essentially in the one province of Connacht. The tradition has Patrick engaging in substantial ministry in northern, central, and eastern Ireland, with some forays beyond. An ancient document called the "Annals of the Four Masters" reports that Patrick's mission planted about 700 churches, and that Patrick ordained perhaps 1000 priests.[29] Within his lifetime, 30 to 40 (or more) of Ireland's 150 tribes became substantially Christian. Louis Gougaud offers this assessment:

> Most certainly he did not succeed in converting all the heathens of the island; but he won so many of them for Christ, he founded so many churches, ordained so many clerics, kindled such a zeal in men's hearts, that it seems right to believe that to him was directly due the wonderful outblossoming of Christianity which distinguished Ireland in the following ages.[30]

Patrick's achievement included social dimensions. He was the first public man to speak and crusade against slavery. Within his lifetime, or soon after, "the Irish slave trade came to a halt, and other forms of violence, such as murder and intertribal warfare decreased," and his communities modeled the Christian way of faithfulness, generosity, and peace to all the Irish.[31]

One would naturally assume that the British Church, which had ordained Patrick a bishop and sent him to Ireland, would continue to affirm his mission and celebrate

its achievements. This was far from the case. The generation of British bishops who succeeded the bishops who
originally sent Patrick did not "own" their predecessor's
appointment. Some of them, perhaps most, criticized him
savagely. This criticism stung Patrick, and aroused him to
write the "Declaration" that defended his ministry.

What was the "beef" of the British Church leaders? They
seem to have defined two roles (only) for a bishop: admin-
istrator and chaplain. Therefore, a bishop's primary (perhaps only) expectations were to administer the existing
churches and care for faithful Christians. (A local priest's
job description was similar, stressing pastoral care of the
local flock.) So the British leaders were offended and
angered that Patrick was spending priority time with
"pagans," "sinners," and "barbarians."

This perspective had surfaced four centuries earlier.
Jesus had been savagely criticized by the Pharisees for
practicing the same kind of fraternizing priorities that
Patrick now practiced. Furthermore, this perspective is
widespread today. Pastors and churches, today, who
regard outreach to lost people as the church's main busi-
ness, and especially those who are perceived to prefer the
company of lost people to the company of church people,
are suspect, marginalized, and "shot at" by establishment
Christians and church leaders. No major denomination in
the United States regards apostolic ministry to pre-
Christian outsiders as its "priority" or even as "normal"
ministry.

Patrick seized the high ground. Implicitly, he reminded
his detractors of what it means to serve in "apostolic suc-
cession," that is, to succeed the ancient apostles in their
mission to pre-Christian populations. Explicitly, he defended his calling in terms of the biblical warrants for priority
outreach to pre-Christian populations. Patrick explains that
he has devoted his life to helping Irish populations be

"reborn in God" and "redeemed from the ends of the earth" because the Church is placed in the world "as a light among the nations" to "fish well" and "to spread our nets so that we can catch a great . . . multitude for God." The Church, he reminded them, is commanded by the risen Christ go into "all the world," and "to preach the gospel to all creation," and to "teach all nations" in anticipation of "the last days" when the Lord "will pour out [his] spirit over all flesh" and make peoples who were not his into "children of the living God." So, Patrick wrote, "this is why it come about in Ireland that people who had no acquaintance with God . . . are recently . . . made a people of the Lord and are known as children of God. . . . For God gave me such grace, that many people through me were reborn to God and afterward confirmed and brought to perfection."[32]

CHAPTER 2

A New Kind of Community, A New Kind of Life

I rish Christianity spread even more in the generations following the death of Patrick than it had in Patrick's own lifetime. Since we have no written records from that period, our knowledge of how the Irish Church grew in its first century is spotty, but two facts are paramount. First, the available evidence suggests that Patrick's movement blanketed the island: "In Ireland alone, there are more than 6,000 place names containing the element Cill—the old Gaelic word for church."[1] Second, Irish Christianity was geographically beyond the reach of Rome's ability to shape and control, so a distinctively Celtic approach to "doing church" and living the Christian life emerged.

What would a visitor from Rome have noticed about Celtic Christianity that was "different"? The visitor would have observed more of a movement than an institution, with small provisional buildings of wood and mud, a movement featuring laity in ministry more than clergy. This movement, compared to the Roman wing of the One Church was more imaginative and less cerebral, closer to nature and its creatures, and emphasized the "immanence" and "providence" of the Triune God more than his "transcendence."

Most of all, the Roman visitor would notice that Patrick's "remarkable achievement was to found a new kind of church, one which broke the Roman imperial mould and was both catholic and barbarian."[2]

That "new kind of church" gradually displaced the

parish church as Irish Christianity's dominant form of Christian community. I call this new kind of church the "monastic community." Patrick's leadership had "indigenized" Christianity to Irish cultural soil more than anyone else was attempting anywhere. Since Patrick refers to "monks" and "virgins for Christ" in his writings, we presume that he and his people started monastic communities in his lifetime. Some writers believe he started monastic communities somewhat like he had observed in Gaul.[3] Patrick emphasized, however, the planting of traditional parish churches, each with a priest, with groups of churches administered by a bishop, which followed the established Roman way of "doing church."

However, the parish church model did not really fit ancient Irish life. The Roman model presupposed an organized town or village, with a parish church at the town's center. It also presupposed a network of towns, connected by roads, within a geographic political unit (like a county) that could double as a bishop's diocese. Celtic Ireland had no established towns however, only temporary settlements of tribal groups. Ireland had no official political units or boundaries. Furthermore, Ireland had few if any roads more useful than a Class B cow trail![4] Much of the "traffic" was confined to sea lanes. A modern visitor who stepped back into fourth century Ireland would observe random, shifting, "rural sprawl" in every direction.

Patrick's successors adopted his principle of indigenous Christianity and extended it. They learned about "monasteries" from Eastern Christianity, perhaps through visits to Gaul and the Eastern Church, and certainly through reading the best selling *Life of St. Anthony* by Athanasius. Then they radically adapted the idea of the monastery to Ireland. The resulting community was so different from many of the eastern monasteries that we need a distinct term such as "monastic communities."

What was the difference between Eastern monasteries and Celtic monastic communities? Briefly, the Eastern monasteries organized to protest and escape from the materialism of the Roman world and the corruption of the Church; the Celtic monasteries organized to penetrate the pagan world and to extend the Church. The eastern monks often withdrew from the world into monasteries to save and cultivate their own souls; Celtic leaders often organized monastic communities to save other people's souls. The leaders of the Eastern monasteries located their monasteries in isolated locations, off the beaten track; the Celtic Christians built their monastic communities in locations accessible to the traffic of the time, like proximity to settlements, or on hilltops, or on islands near the established sea lanes.[5]

Celtic monastic communities did include some monks and/or nuns who lived disciplined ascetic lives; such monks and nuns often founded monastic communities, but Celtic communities were much more diverse than eastern monasteries. They were also populated by priests, teachers, scholars, craftsmen, artists, farmers, families, and children, as well as monks and/or nuns—all under the leadership of a lay abbot or a lay abbess.[6] They had little use for more than a handful of ordained priests, or for people seeking ordination; they were essentially lay movements. Some monastic communities contained more than one thousand people; a few, such as Bangor and Clonfert, may have been as large as three thousand people.

Within the threefold division of the day into worship, study, and work, monastic communities were beehives of a wide range of activities. John Finney observes that "there would have been little of the monastic peace that pervades modern communities and [the] monks went outside the enclosure when they wanted peace and quiet."[7] With some variation from one community to another, children went to school, young men and women prepared for Christian vocations, and Christian scholarship was fostered.[8] Some inhabitants copied decaying books onto new parchments, others "illuminated" the scriptures, and others practiced other arts and crafts.[9] Other people herded cows; or sheared sheep; or made cloth; or cultivated crops; or cooked for the community; or cared for sick people, or sick animals, or guests. The community worshiped together, perhaps twice daily; they learned much of the scriptures together—by heart, especially the psalms. They nourished each other in a life of "contemplative prayer," and many monastic communities also functioned as "mission stations," preparing people for mission to unreached populations.[10]

Some of the ways in which a Celtic community differed from an Eastern cloistered monastery would have been obvious to any sojourner. The visitor would first pass beyond a circular outer wall and through a gate that signified one was entering hallowed ground. The wall did not signify an enclosure to keep out the world; the area signified the "alternative" way of life, free of aggression and violence and devoted to God's purposes that the community modeled for the world. Philip Sheldrake tells us that

> This enclosure, or *termon*, was to be a place free from all aggression. Violence was legally and absolutely excluded by this precinct. . . . Monastic settlements [were] anticipations of paradise in which the forces of division, violence and evil were excluded. Wild beasts were tamed and nature was regulated. The privileges of Adam and Eve in Eden, received from God but lost by the Fall, were reclaimed. The living out of this vision of an alternative world involved all the people who were brought within the enclosed space.[11]

Once past the enclosure, the visitor would notice (say, as at Glendalough) a porter's dwelling, a cathedral, several chapels, a round tower, one or more tall stone Celtic crosses, a cemetery, a well, the abbot's house, a guest house, many small cells for one or two people, larger dwellings for families, a kitchen, a refectory, a scriptorium, a library, workshops, farm land, grazing land, etc. The visitor would especially notice the guest house. Sheldrake informs us that

> guests . . . were accorded a kind of semi-spiritual status and housed within the sacred enclosure. Often the guest house was given the choicest site within the settlement and yet was always set apart, sometimes within its own enclosure. The *hospitium*, therefore, was within the sacred space (isolated from the outside world) yet separated from the monastic living quarters. The guest quarters was itself, therefore, a kind of "boundary place" between two worlds.[12]

The geography and architecture of the monastic community would appear quite planned and organized—in two or more concentric circles. The perceptive visitor would appreciate that the Celtic Christian movement had *created* community in the midst of rural sprawl!

There are two ways (at least) in which these unusual communities produced an unusual approach to the living out of Christianity, compared to the Roman form. First, the monastic communities produced a less individualistic and more community-oriented approach to the Christian life. This affected the way in which—in parish churches, communities, tribes, and families—the people supported each other, pulled together, prayed for each other, worked out their salvation together, and lived out the Christian life together. Every person had multiple role models for living as a Christian and, in a more profound and pervasive sense than on the continent, Irish Christians knew what it meant to be a Christian family or tribe. (Chapter 4 expands upon the Celtic movement's communal approach to Christianity.)

Second, Celtic Christianity addressed a "zone" of human concern that Western Christianity, and other world religions, have generally ignored. Paul Heibert, in a classic article called "The Flaw of the Excluded Middle," shows how the earth's peoples explain life, live life, and face the future at three levels.[13] The bottom level deals with the factors in life that our senses can apprehend; this is the "empirical" world that the "sciences" deal with. At this level, people learn to plant a crop, to clean a fish, to fix a water pump, to build a house, and a thousand other things. The top level deals with the ultimate issues in life that are beyond what our senses can perceive; this is a "transcendent" or "sacred" realm that Christianity and the other world religions define, and then address. Heibert reports that "religion as a system of explanation deals with the ultimate questions of the origin, purpose, and destiny of an individual, a society, and the universe."[14] Western society and the Western churches, especially since the Enlightenment, have tended to exclude from their view of reality a middle level that is nevertheless quite real to people in most societies (and increasingly real to postmodern people in the West).

What are the "middle-level" issues of life? Here one finds the questions of the uncertainty of the near future, the crises of present life, and the unknowns of the past. Despite knowledge of facts such as that seeds once planted will grow and bear fruit, or that travel down this river on a boat will bring one to the neighboring village, the future is not totally predictable. Accidents, misfortunes, the intervention of other persons, and other unknown events can frustrate human planning.[15]

For many peoples, Heibert adds, this middle realm is inhabited by "mechanical" forces such as mana, spells, omens, evil eye, or luck, and/or by more "organic" presences like spirits, ghosts, ancestors, angels, demons, lesser gods, etc. In their traditional folk religions people turn to, say, the local shaman (who can influence these middle-level forces) for a fruitful marriage, or safety during travel, or for protection from evil eye or bad luck.[16]

The problem is that Western Christianity usually ignores this middle level that drives most people's lives most of the time, as do the other world religions. Western Christian leaders usually focus on the "ultimate" issues, as they define them, to the exclusion of the lesser issues; indeed, they often consider middle issues "beneath" them! When Christianity ignores, or does not help people cope with, these middle issues, we often observe "Split-Level Christianity" in which people go to church so they can go to heaven, but they also visit, say, the shaman or the astrologer for help with the pressing problems that dominate their daily lives.

Celtic Christians had no need to seek out a shaman. Their Christian faith and community addressed life as a whole and may have addressed the middle level more specifically, comprehensively, and powerfully than any other Christian movement ever has. A folk Christianity of, by, and for the people developed. It helped common people to live and cope as Christians day by day in the face of poverty, enemies, evil forces, nature's uncertainties, and frequent threats from many quarters. This folk Christianity can be seen today in the people's prayers and blessings that were passed on orally for many generations. In the nineteenth century, Douglas Hyde interviewed many keepers of the Christian folk tradition in Ireland, and Alexander Carmichael collected such lore in the Hebrides Islands. Carmichael's *Carmina Gadelica* was originally published in five volumes.[17] Reading through the *Carmina Gadelica* gives one a deeper appreciation of the "contemplative prayer" that characterized Celtic Christian piety.

Ray Simpson, in *Exploring Celtic Spirituality*, explains that contemplative prayer contrasts with the more usual approach of praying at a specific time or meeting, and it contrasts with the more usual petitionary approach that "requests God to do specific things." Indeed, it is "the opposite of controlling prayer." Contemplative prayer is the way we fulfill St. Paul's counsel to "pray without ceasing."[18] It is an ongoing, or very frequent, opening of the heart to the Triune God, often while engaging in each of the many experiences that fill a day.

The *Carmina Gadelica* tradition gave people brief *daily rituals*, which they learned by heart, with suggested affirmations or prayers for directing their hearts, moment by moment, setting by setting. The Celtic Christians learned prayers to accompany getting up in the morning, for dressing, for starting the morning fire, for bathing or washing clothes or dishes, for "smooring" the fire at days end, and for going to bed at night. One for starting the morning fire begins

> I will kindle my fire this morning
> In presence of the holy angles of heaven,
> God, kindle Thou in my heart within
> A flame of love to my neighbor,
> To my foe, to my friend, to my kindred all,
> To the brave, to the knave, to the thrall . . . .[19]

The *Carmina Gadelica* taught people how to pray for sowing seed and for harvesting crops; for herding cows or milking cows or churning butter; for before a meal and after; for a sprain or a toothache; for a new baby or a new baby chick. Celtic Christians prayed while weaving, hunting, fishing, cooking, or traveling. They knew prayers for the healing of many conditions including blindness, warts, bruises, swollen breasts, and chest seizure.

The *Carmina Gadelica* taught Celtic parents lullabies to sing to their children at night. It gave people affirmations to prepare themselves for prayer, such as

> I am bending my knee
> In the eye of the Father who created me,
> In the eye of the Son who purchased me,
> In the eye of the Spirit who cleansed me,
> In friendship and affection.[20]

Many of the invocations, prayers, and blessings in the *Carmina Gadelica* employ repetition, and are thoroughly Trinitarian, as in the following prayer.

> I lie down this night with God,
> And God will lie down with me;
> I lie down this night with Christ,
> And Christ will lie down with me;
> I lie down this night with the Spirit,
> And the Spirit will lie down with me;
> God and Christ and the Spirit
> Be lying down with me.[21]

As we explore more thoroughly in chapter 4, the Celtic style of prayer engages people's imaginations through visual and spatial imagery.

> The Three Who are over me,
> The Three who are below me,
> The Three Who are above me here,
> The Three who are above me yonder;
> The Three Who are in the earth,
> The Three Who are in the air,
> The Three who are in the heavens,
> The Three Who are in the great pouring sea.[22]

Many of the subjects in the *Carmina Gadelica* are, of course, dated. Today, most people never smoor a fire or churn butter or shear a sheep.

Ray Simpson, in his book *Celtic Blessings for Everyday Life*,[23] has updated the Celtic contemplative prayer approach for this generation. For instance, Simpson has prayers for when one gets a new car, or a bicycle, or a motorcycle, or a new job. There are prayers for journeying by car or for working at one's computer. One finds prayers for the transitions of life—going to school, leaving school, leaving home, falling in love, mid-life crisis, and retirement. He features prayers for anniversaries and reunions, for divorce, for infertility and miscarriage, for stepchildren, for battered people and victims of crime. Simpson even includes a prayer for taking an exam!

Exams

> I bless this exam
> in the name of the Designer of truth.
> I bless this exam
> in the name of the Protector from ill.
> I bless this exam
> in the name of the Spirit who guides.
> Open my eyes to see how this subject
> reflects something of you.
> Aid me to understand this subject
> with my heart as well as with my head.
> Give me
> Wisdom to know the nub of things,
> Strength to recall what is useful,
> Peace to leave the result to you.[24]

The Celtic Christian Movement proceeded to multiply mission-sending monastic communities, which continued to send teams into settlements to multiply churches and start people in the community-based life of full devotion to the Triune God. This movement was fueled by "the burning zeal of the apostles of the country," and "their aim was wonderfully furthered by the ardent temperament of the newly won converts."[25] In two or three generations, all of Ireland had become substantially Christian and, as we will see in the next chapter, Celtic monastic communities became the strategic "mission stations" from which apostolic bands reached the "barbarians" of Scotland, and much of England, and much of Western Europe.

CHAPTER 3

To the Picts, the Anglo-Saxons, and Other "Barbarians"

ithin a century after Patrick's death, Irish Celtic Christians were lifting their eyes to see harvests beyond Ireland. In A.D. 563, an entourage accompanied Columba,[1] a formidable apostolic leader, to the island called Iona, off of Scotland's west coast, which would serve as the primary base for reaching the Picts of Scotland. The size of his entourage—20 bishops, 40 priests, 30 deacons, and 50 students—suggests his seriousness.[2] Again, with appropriate adaptations for reaching people of a somewhat different culture, Celtic Christian leaders paid the price to understand the Picts, their language, and their culture; they multiplied monastic communities which sent out teams to engage settlements and plant churches. Within a century, the Picts were substantially Christian.

By the early seventh century, the demographics of northern and central England had changed. Swarms of Angles, Saxons, Jutes, and other Germanic peoples, (known, collectively, as "Anglo-Saxons") invaded the land and drove many of the Britons to Brittany (where they became known as "Bretons"), or to Wales (where they became known as the "Welsh"). The Britons who stayed were absorbed into Anglo-Saxon culture. In A.D. 633, Iona commissioned an entourage led by Aidan to establish a monastic community on a tidal island called Lindisfarne, off the coast of northeast England. Ian Bradley observes that Aidan's community "was to prove almost as important a missionary centre as its mother house at Iona. From it monks penetrated far down into the areas of England held by the pagan Angles and Saxons."[3]

The mission of Aidan and his people represented the third major strategic adjustment in the history of Celtic Christian expansion. Patrick and his people, who were Romanized Britons from England, had adapted their mission to fit the culture of the pagan Irish Celts. Columba and his people, all Irish, had adjusted to the somewhat different language and culture of the Celtic Picts in Scotland. Now Aidan and his entourage, most of them Irish, were in cross-cultural mission to the Germanic Anglo-Saxons now populating England—people with a very different language, culture, and primal religion. Henry Mayr-Harting explains that, "As all the Germanic peoples had issued ultimately from Scandinavia, so they shared a common stock of mythology with the Scandinavians."[4] Again, the missionaries labored to understand this very different population.

In broad outline, the emerging strategy of Aidan and his people looks familiar. First, they multiplied monastic communities. We have no way of knowing how many such communities the movements spawned by Patrick, Columba, Aidan and others established in the British Isles alone. John Finney cites evidence showing thirty-two monastic communities in the area of Worcester; that density would indicate many hundreds, or even thousands, of monastic communities across the British Isles.[5]

Second, they sent apostolic teams from monastic communities to reach settlements within the region. Finney observes that the monastic community was led by an abbot or abbess, while the apostolic team was often led by a bishop. In the Celtic Christian movement, "the bishops performed the sacramental actions peculiar to their order, such as ordination, but above all were the leaders of evangelistic missions into the surrounding countryside and to the local secular leadership."[6] The team would engage in sustained group visits to settlements where they would minister with the people, interpret the gospel in indigenous ways, and plant churches. Aidan and his people were able to build on the efforts of Paulinus (and others) who preceded them in Northumbria.[7] Nevertheless, the Anglo-Saxons were not reached easily. Mayr-Harting reports that

> The Anglo-Saxons . . . were not converted at all quickly. . . . It took nearly 90 years to convert just the kings and the greater part of their aristocracy, not to speak of the countryside which was a question of centuries. In the course of that near-90 years hardly a court was converted which did not suffer at least one subsequent relapse into paganism before being reconverted.[8]

Meanwhile, in this same period, another mission was launched in the south of England, at Canterbury. Pope Gregory, with a vision to make "angels" of the "Angles," commissioned a librarian named Augustine and forty other monks to England. These missionaries of the Roman Christian tradition arrived in A.D. 597, and in time their movement experienced some success. Essentially, they succeeded in reaching several peoples in the south of England, largely south of the Thames.[9] The Roman tradition regards Augustine as "The Apostle of England." While Augustine's work began in A.D. 597, and Aidan's not until A.D. 633, the movement of Aidan expanded so much more and reached so many of the peoples of northern and central England, a stronger case can be made for Aidan being "The Apostle of England."

In the period in which England's demographics were changing due to the Anglo-Saxon occupation, the demographics of Western Europe were changing even more. "Barbarian" Germanic populations like the Goths had pressured and invaded the Roman Empire for decades while, from multiple causes, the empire was also crumbling from within.[10] Rome itself fell to a military invasion in A.D. 410, and a series of events occurred that would, in time, usher in "the Dark Ages"—in which the "barbarian" hoards largely destroyed the arts, architecture, and (especially) the libraries of Roman Civilization.

Meanwhile, back in Ireland, the Irish Christian leaders were convinced that they had learned something about reaching "barbarians" with the gospel. Indeed, they now believed they were a people chosen by God for mission to the "barbarians" of Western Europe. An Irish apostle named Columbanus, with entourage, departed for Europe in A.D. 600 to launch a Celtic Christian mission to the continent. He may not have been the first Irish apostle to Europe, "but he was certainly the pioneer who inspired the mass exodus later."[11] Irish missionaries in Europe faced the threefold challenge of converting "barbarian" peoples to Christianity, and converting Arian "barbarians" to orthodox Christianity, and renewing Christian populations who had "fallen into laxity and immorality."[12] In the next fifteen years, Columbanus founded monastic communities in (what is now) France, Switzerland, and Italy; and in time his people founded a vast network of sixty or more monastic communities, learned a dozen or more languages and cultures, engaged peoples, planted churches, and launched a significant Christian movement among the barbarian peoples of Europe, particularly in (what is now) France, Belgium, Switzerland, Austria, Germany, and Italy. In the first half of the eighth century, Boniface—an Anglo-Saxon mission leader employing (more or less) Celtic methods of mission—provided an additional generation of leadership that, in time, enabled the Germanic peoples of Europe to become substantially Christian.

Through several generations of sustained mission, Celtic Christianity thus reevangelized Europe, helped bring

Europe out of the Dark Ages, fueled Charlemagne's Carolingian Renaissance, and ushered in the "Holy Roman Empire." Even those Celtic Christians who did not venture out, but stayed at the monasteries, played an indispensable role. By laboring in their *scriptoria* to copy the learning of the past onto new parchment, they preserved for posterity much of the classic literature of Greece and Rome. That, in the words of Thomas Cahill, is "How the Irish Saved Civilization!" While the Roman branch of the Church had long stopped growing, the mission of the Celtic branch had rescued Western civilization and restored movemental Christianity in Europe.

You would think that the Roman wing of the Church would have been grateful for the expansion achieved by the mission of the Celtic wing and, begrudgingly, it was; but the Roman wing's leaders repeatedly criticized the Celtic wing for not doing church the "Roman way!" The two wings of the Church came into focused conflict at the Synod of Whitby in A.D. 664, called by the regional King Oswiu.[13] They clashed over two apparently superficial issues: 1) By their contrasting method of calculating the date for Easter, the Celtic churches were often celebrating Easter on a different date than Rome prescribed. 2) The hairstyle of the Celtic priests and monks contrasted with the "tonsure" of Roman priests and monks. The two sides expounded their views at the Synod of Whitby. The Romans arrived better organized and, once again, the lions defeated the tigers. King Oswiu sided with the Roman case and ruled that the Roman approach should replace the Celtic approach everywhere. In A.D. 670, a synod at Autun in France ruled that the Celtic monastic communities across Europe had to adopt the (Roman) Benedictine rule.[14]

The real issues, of course, ran deeper than hairstyle, a date for Easter, and norms for community life. One issue was conservatism versus change. The Celtic Christians used a more ancient method for calculating the date of Easter than did the Romans; in that practice, and many others, they had not adopted Rome's innovations. David Bosch once observed that "By and large, . . . Catholicism endorsed the principle that a 'missionary church' must reflect in every detail the Roman custom of the moment."[15]

A second issue was indigeneity versus cultural uniformity. In the hairstyle matter, and many others, Celtic Christianity had adapted to the people's culture; the Romans wanted Roman cultural forms imposed upon *all* churches and peoples—a policy that was alien to the Celtic movement's practice and genius.

The driving issue, of course, was control. That is why it was so important, to the Romans, for everyone to do church the "Roman way." Once any society accepted Christianity, the politically dominant Roman wing of the Church insisted that the young churches organize in the Roman pattern of dioceses led by bishops and learn to worship in Latin, follow the liturgy from Rome, sing the music from Rome, etc.

The Synods of Whitby and Autun presumably settled the matter: the Roman way should be followed everywhere. In some cases, Celtic priests who refused to do church the Roman way were banished; in other cases, Benedictine rule was forced on Celtic monasteries.[16] More often, presumably, church and secular leaders simply pressured Celtic leaders to conform, and they praised and rewarded those who did. Within two centuries of the Synods at Whitby and Autun, the Roman way largely prevailed throughout the Western Church. Nora Chadwick observes that

> the disappearance of the idiosyncratic Christianity of the Celtic Church was inevitable, owing to the absence of central organization; but it is impossible to reach the end without a feeling of regret. A Christianity so pure and so serene as that of the age of the saints could hardly be equaled and never repeated.[17]

Bede's history of the monasteries at Wearmouth and Jarrow, in northeast England, is a local edition of this wider history.[18] Bede's version of this local history begins with the story of the abbot Benedict, who

> went to Rome, where, in fulfillment of his long and ardent desire, he made sure he visited the tombs of the apostles and venerated their remains. Directly he returned home he devoted himself wholeheartedly and unceasingly to making known as widely as possible the forms of church life which he had seen in Rome and had come to love and cherish.[19]

Doing church the Roman way was Benedict's obsession (and, transparently, Bede's as well). Bede's history of the two monasteries reports frequent travel, by abbots and monks, to and from Rome. They visited shrines in Rome, they observed how churches in Rome were "doing church," and they sent their bishop to be consecrated in Rome. They stocked their libraries with books from Rome. They brought paintings and sacred relics from Rome. They built a "stone church in the Roman style."[20] At one point, Benedict brought from Rome a choirmaster named John, who "taught the monks at first hand how things were done in the churches in Rome."[21]

For the record, Bede and the other Roman Christian leaders were not prejudicial toward Celtic culture only, nor were they engaged in selective discrimination against Celtic ways; they assumed that Roman ways were superior to the ways of *all* other cultures. Furthermore, they were supremely confident that Christianity could only be adequately expressed in Roman cultural forms.

One case reveals these convictions with irrefutable clarity. Bede reports an event in which the pope consecrated Theodore, a Greek, to serve as a bishop in Britain.[22] An abbot, Hadrian, was assigned to accompany, coach, and mentor Theodore until he had internalized Roman ways. The purpose of Hadrian's assignment was "to prevent Theodore from introducing into the church over which he presided any Greek customs which might be contrary to the true faith."[23]

So Bede reports and applauds, *ad nauseam,* the ways in which the monasteries of Wearmouth and Jarrow learned to do everything as in Rome. The rule had changed from "When in Rome, do as the Romans do," to "When anywhere, do as the Romans do!" Notice that by Bede's account, neither Wearmouth nor Jarrow engaged in any mission to pagan populations nor in any ministry or witness to seekers outside or inside either monastery. Wearmouth and Jarrow adopted the Roman forms and the Eastern agenda; their monks experienced the community's Roman ways in order to save their own souls.

Something like the Wearmouth and Jarrow experiences took place almost everywhere and, almost everywhere, the more Roman the monastic communities and churches became, the less they engaged in evangelization. Consequently, "the Celtic Church" became history, although cultural enclaves of Celtic folk Christianity have continued in areas of Ireland, Wales, Cornwall, Scotland, and the Hebrides Islands until today. But the heroic Celtic era of mission ended, and Christianity's apostolic mission was negligible for centuries—until its revival, half a millennium later, in the Counter-Reformation. Not until the Renaissance and Reformation would indigenous languages, cultures, and religious expressions resurface across Europe. Not until Vatican II would the Roman Catholic Church affirm the idea of indigenous Christianity.

Throughout Bede's *Ecclesiastical History,* the nongrowing (Roman) wing of the Church always assumed that it knew better than the growing (Celtic) wing, and the nongrowing wing worked overtime to control the growing wing and make it conform. By the time the nongrowing wing succeeded in dominating the growing wing, however, the latter had reached the West for a second time.

I have reported at length on the ancient Roman ecclesiastical campaign to control the growing Celtic movement because we observe a parallel case today in most of the "mainline" denominations of the United States, especially those denominations once "born in Europe" and historically exported to North America.

In most American denominations, including mine, the people who control the denomination (or at least control the agenda of the denomination) are the same people who are less apostolic in their emphasis; who assume that they know best; who put in the most overtime to gain and retain influence in the denomination, and are certain that a *European* way of doing church is best for all churches. Their special obsession is to control the growing wing of the church and "correct" it in a European direction! (The model has shifted in one important way. A thousand years ago, Church executives pressured churches to do church in current ways that reflected the Roman customs of the moment. Today, executives expect the churches to do church in traditional European ways, while complying with the hierarchy's political views of the moment!)

For many decades, a European model for American churches was reasonably effective, because the USA moved through history more or less in tandem with Europe until, say, the 1920s—when Western Europe and North America moved, increasingly, in different directions. Today, as Lyle Schaller has demonstrated, the preponderance of denominations "imported from Europe" are declining while the preponderance of churches "made in America" are growing.[24]

Why that should make a significant difference may not be obvious, but is easily demonstrated. For example, the architecture of an "imported from Europe" (IFE) church is usually Western European; the architecture of a "made in America" (MIA) church is usually functional and open. IFE liturgical language is usually rooted in European past; MIA liturgical language is usually current American English. IFE beliefs and worship traditions usually emphasize the first person of the Trinity; MIA beliefs and worship traditions usually emphasize the second or third person of the Trinity.

More specifically, IFE churches usually feature acoustic sounds and music composed before 1960 (or 1760!); MIA churches are more likely to feature electronic sounds and music composed after 1960 (or 1980). The worship of IFE churches is usually formal, developed for believers, with the goal of "proper worship"; the worship of MIA churches is more likely to be informal, developed with seekers in mind, with the goals of meeting people's religious needs and changing lives.

IFE denominations usually have a hierarchical organization, which produces programs for the churches and expects people to trust the system; MIA denominations more likely have a flatter organization, which works more responsively with churches, and expects the system to trust the people. IFE churches usually think of the church as the real estate and have low expectations of the members; MIA churches more often think of the church as the people, and they have high expectations for the people. Churches "made in America" are much more likely to give people choices, to be future oriented, to affirm entrepreneurs and new ideas, and to start new ministries and new churches than churches "imported from Europe."[25] In other words, the Protestant Reformation left the Control-from-Rome paradigm essentially unchallenged. For Protestants, the locus of control merely shifted from Rome to Wittenberg or Geneva or Canterbury, and then to New York or Chicago or

Nashville. Most of the Europe-oriented leaders of America's "mainline" denominations are in denial, however, and they continue to assume that control from headquarters and the culturally European paradigm are best for churches everywhere.

As I write this, these very issues have surfaced in the 1998 meeting of the World Council of Churches in Harare, Zimbabwe. Christianity is now growing rapidly in Africa; Roman Catholicism has doubled in twenty years; Lutherans have grown by two-thirds in seven years. However, the continual pressure for African churches to do church in European (and American) ways has caused the rise of many "African Independent Churches,"who insist on the right to do church in African ways for Africans, and who are now growing much more than the African denominations still tied to Euro-American denominations. In the Harare meeting, however, African theologians (!) advocated more culturally African ways for Africans, claiming that worship should engage Africans emotionally as well as intellectually. They observed that many "churches have grown by embracing African forms of worship, sacred music and dance, and by moving away from styles linked with former colonial rulers."[26]

CHAPTER 4

The Celtic Christian Community in Formation and Mission

hat can now be known about *how* Celtic Christianity "won the West" for the second time? The rest of this book attempts to unpack the multiple "strategic causes" for Celtic Christian expansion. This chapter focuses on how the Celtic way of "being and doing church" contributed to the reevangelization of Europe in the centuries before the Roman way eclipsed the Celtic Way. Five themes suggest what we might learn about "missionary ecclesiology" from the ancient Celtic Christian movement.

First, in significant contrast to contemporary Christianity's well-known evangelism approaches of "Lone Ranger" one-to-one evangelism, or confrontational evangelism, or the public preaching crusade, (and in stark contrast to contemporary Christianity's more dominant approach of not reaching out at all!), we have already seen how the Celtic Christians usually evangelized as a team—by relating to the people of a settlement; identifying with the people; engaging in friendship, conversation, ministry, and witness—with the goal of raising up a church in measurable time. John Finney observes that the Celts believed in "the importance of the team. A group of people can pray and think together. They inspire and encourage each other. The single entrepreneur is too easily prey to self doubt and loss of vision."[1]

The second theme focuses on how the monastic community prepared people to live with depth, compassion, and power in mission. Celtic Christianity seems to have prepared people through a fivefold structure of experiences. (1) You experienced voluntary periods of solitary isolation, ordinarily in a primitive cell erected within a remote natural setting—like a grove of trees near a stream. Drawing on the wisdom of the desert fathers and mothers of the Eastern Church, Celtic leaders advised you to "Go, sit in your cell, and your cell will teach you everything."[2] (2) You spent time with your *anamchara*, that is, your "soul friend"—not a superior like a "spiritual director," but a peer with whom you were vulnerable and accountable; to whom you made confession; from whom you received penance; who both supported and challenged you.[3] (3) If the monastic community was at all large, you spent time with a small group of ten or fewer people—led by someone chosen primarily for their devotion.[4] (4) You participated in the common life, meals, work, learning, biblical recitation, prayers, and worship of the whole monastic community. (5) Through your small group, and the community's life, and perhaps as a soul friend, you observed and gained experience in ministry and witness to pre-Christian people. The community's purposes for you, through this fivefold structure, were to root your consciousness in the gospel and the scriptures; to help you experience the presence of the Triune God and an empowered life; to help you discover and fulfill your vocation; and to give you experience in ministry with seekers.

A third theme, weaving through the second, focuses on the role of *imaginative prayer* in all the settings—in solitude, with the soul friend, in the small group, in the corporate life, and in ministry with seekers—of life within the monastic community. We will see, in chapter 5, that Celtic evangelization took people's "right brains" seriously; they made the gospel's meaning vivid, and engaged people's feelings, and energized their response by engaging their imaginations.

The Celts' affirmation of human imagination also shaped the legendary Celtic life of prayer. Esther de Waal is a contemporary champion of activating the religious imagination for meaningful prayer.[5] She defines the Christian life as a journey, in the company of other pilgrims and the Triune God, with dark forces about us and the saints pulling for us. The imaginative style of prayer that fuels this life typically focuses on space and images, attaining a visual quality, and is characterized by cogency and poetic repetition. De Wall explains:

> Above all the Celtic tradition has reminded me of the importance of images, those foundational images whose depths and universal character have always brought such riches to Christian understanding. . . . It now becomes vital more than ever, to recover the fundamental images of fire, wind, bread, water, of light and dark, of the heart. These are the great impersonal symbols which are universal, understood by Christian and nonchristian alike.[6]

The Psalms, of course, have these features, and Celtic Christians often sang and prayed thirty psalms a day. However, the Celtic Christians also wrote new prayers and many have been passed on for centuries. This part of a prayer serves as an example of cogency and poetic repetition.

> O Father who sought me
> O Son who bought me
> O Holy Spirit who taught me.[7]

The most famous Celtic prayer, "St. Patrick's Breastplate," stands as a magnificent example of the visual quality of many Celtic prayers.

> I rise today
> in power's strength, invoking the Trinity,
> believing in threeness,
> confessing the oneness,
> of creation's Creator.

I rise today
  in the power of Christ's birth and baptism,
  in the power of his crucifixion and burial,
  in the power of his rising and ascending,
  in the power of his descending and judging.

I rise today
  in the power of the love of cherubim,
  in the obedience of angels,
  and service of archangels,
  in hope of rising to receive the reward,
  in the prayers of patriarchs,
  in the predictions of prophets,
  in the preaching of apostles,
  in the faith of confessors,
  in the innocence of holy virgins,
  in the deeds of the righteous.

I rise today
  in heavens might,
  in sun's brightness,
  in moon's radiance,
  in fire's glory,
  in lightning's quickness,
  in wind's swiftness,
  in sea's depth,
  in earth's stability,
  in rock's fixity.

I rise today
  with the power of God to pilot me,
  God's strength to sustain me,
  God's wisdom to guide me,
  God's eye to look ahead for me,
  God's ear to hear me,
  God's word to speak for me,
  God's hand to protect me,
  God's way before me,
  God's shield to defend me,
  God's host to deliver me:
        from snares of devils,

from evil temptations,
from nature's failings,
from all who wish to harm me,
far or near,
alone and in a crowd.

Around me I gather today all these powers
against every cruel and merciless force
to attack my body and soul,
against the charms of false prophets,
the black laws of paganism,
the false laws of heretics
the deceptions of idolatry,
against spells cast by women, smiths and druids,
and all unlawful knowledge
that harms the body and soul.

May Christ protect me today
against poison and burning,
against drowning and wounding,
so that I may have abundant reward;
Christ with me, Christ before me, Christ behind me;
Christ within me, Christ beneath me, Christ above me,
Christ to right of me, Christ to left of me;
Christ in my lying, Christ in my sitting,
    Christ in my rising;
Christ in the heart of all who think of me.
Christ on the tongue of all who speak to me,
Christ in the eye of all who see me,
Christ in the ear of all who hear me.

I rise today
in power's strength, invoking the Trinity,
believing in threeness,
confessing the oneness,
of creation's Creator.

For to the Lord belongs salvation,
and to the Lord belongs salvation
and to Christ belongs salvation
May your salvation, Lord, be with us always.[8]

The fourth theme is the role of the monastic community's Hospitality in ministry with seekers, visitors, refugees, and other "guests." We have seen that one Celtic approach to pre-Christian people involved a team from the monastic community penetrating the natural community of the target population. We now feature the approach of inviting seekers, refugees and others, individuals and even families, to be guests of the monastic community.

Put yourself in the place of a seeker, or a refugee, or an abused teenager, who has been invited to visit a monastic community, and you have found your way there. What would you likely experience?[9] You would meet a "porter" stationed near the monastic community's entrance, whose chief role is to welcome guests and introduce them to the rest of the community.[10] The abbot, and everyone else, would welcome you with "all courtesy of love." The abbot would gently inquire about what had prompted your visit (and so begin the ministry of conversation), and he would read a scripture for you, offer a prayer for you, and extend the "kiss of peace." The abbot would wash your feet (from your journey by foot), and would show you to the guest house—which would be managed by a caring brother who would give you bedding. You would be included at the Abbot's table at meals; if the Abbot was in a period of fasting, he would break the fast—for the Abbot has no higher priority than ministry with guests. You would learn that the monastic community's highest commitment is hospitality to strangers, seekers, pilgrims, and refugees. The Benedictine Rule #53 explains that "All guests who present themselves are to be welcomed as Christ, for he himself will say: 'I was a stranger and you welcomed me.' "

Soon you would be given a soul friend, a small group, and a place for periods of solitude. You would learn some scripture; you would worship with the community. One or more persons would share the ministry of conversation and pray with you, daily. After some days, or weeks, you would find yourself believing what these Christians believe, and they would invite you to commit your life to Christ and his will for your life.

The fifth and final theme follows from the fourth and focuses more explicitly on the role of the seeker's experience of the Christian community in the process of conversion. This theme represents the major contribution of John Finney's pioneering book *Recovering the Past: Celtic and Roman Mission*.[11] Finney's book does us the service of contrasting the Roman way of doing mission and evangelism vis-à-vis the Celtic way.

Bluntly stated, the Roman model for reaching people (who are "civilized" enough) is: (1) Present the Christian message; (2) Invite them to decide to believe in Christ and become Christians; and (3) If they decide positively, welcome them into the church and its fellowship. The Roman model seems very logical to us because most American evangelicals are scripted by it! We explain the gospel, they accept Christ, we welcome them into the church! Presentation, Decision, Assimilation. What could be more logical than that?

But you already know enough to infer the (contrasting) Celtic model for reaching people: (1) You *first* establish community with people, or bring them into the fellowship of your community of faith. (2) Within fellowship, you engage in conversation, ministry, prayer, and worship. (3) In time, as they discover that they now believe, you invite them to commit.

We can contrast the two models on a chart:

Roman Model	*Celtic Model*
Presentation	Fellowship
Decision	Ministry and Conversations
Fellowship	Belief, Invitation to Commitment

The Celtic model reflects the adage that, for most people," Christianity is more caught than taught!"

Years ago, I began discovering the Celtic approach in my field research with converts out of secularity into faith. In interviews, I usually ask new believers: "When did you feel like you really belonged, that you were *wanted* and *welcomed* and *included* in the fellowship of this church?" More and more converts, including a majority of "boomer" converts and a large majority of "buster" converts, comment that they felt like that *before* they believed, and before they officially joined. Indeed, many new believers report that the experience of the fellowship *enabled* them to believe and to commit. For many people, the faith is about three-fourths caught and one-fourth taught.

My cautious conclusions about how most people become Christians were reinforced by a more empirical study sponsored by the United Bible Societies in Great Britain, led and written by John Finney. A research team received 360 completed questionnaires from converts, and they interviewed 151 converts. These 511 converts represented the range of denominations in England, from Anglican and Roman Catholic, to "Free Churches" and the "New Churches." In *Finding Faith Today: How Does It Happen?*[12] Finney reports that most people experience the faith through relationships, that they encounter the gospel through a community of faith, that becoming a Christian involves a process that takes time. In his later book, *Recovering the Past*, Finney summarizes their chief finding in four words. For most people, "belonging comes before believing."

Finney and others believe that we are now rediscovering the approach to mission first pioneered by ancient Celtic Christianity. Finney contends that the Celtic way is more effective with postmodern Western populations than the Roman Way (and its more recent version—the traditional evangelical way). His data shows that more people come to faith gradually (the Celtic model) than suddenly (the Roman model). Furthermore, the ongoing contagious common life of the congregation that permits people to discover faith for themselves, at their own pace, now appears to be much more influential than special event-preaching evangelism. Finney outlines the typical journey of faith that most people experience today:[13]

1. X is introduced into the church through a member of their family, through friendship with some Christians or through a minister;
2. they begin to ask questions;
3. they are invited to explore further and come to a knowledge and practice of the faith (often this is through a nurture group or some form of catechumenate);
4. they discover they have become a Christian, and mark it publicly through baptism or confirmation or whatever is appropriate to their denomination.

Finney cites Professor Robin Gill's observation that, for most people, "belonging comes before believing." For this reason, evangelism is now about "helping people to belong so that they can believe." Finney believes that, as we adapt to a changing Western culture, we will observe a widespread shift from a Roman to a Celtic model.

CHAPTER 5

How Celtic Christianity Communicated the Gospel

 e have seen that the Celtic monastic communities, and teams from these communities, engaged and reached pre-Christian populations who, in many cases, had no prior knowledge of Christianity's message, and were widely thought to be unreachable. We have suggested that understanding the target populations was indispensable, that the people were more responsive when they knew they were understood and that, when seekers were welcomed into the fellowship, the faith was "more caught than taught."

We now address this important question: *How* did the Celtic Christian movement communicate the gospel so effectively to the "barbarian" populations in Ireland, Scotland, England, and Western Europe? Although "no one can say 'Jesus is Lord' except by the Holy Spirit," several perspectives in the field of Communication Theory help us to perceive what the Celtic Christians were doing that helped communicate the meaning of the Christian message.

Aristotle, in his *Rhetoric*, which was published more than three centuries before Christ, observed effective (and ineffective) speakers in various settings and wrote the earliest comprehensive volume of rhetorical theory.[1] He defined rhetoric as "an ability, in each [particular] case, to see the available means of persuasion."[2] Essentially, Aristotle theorized that persuasion takes place in an interplay between the *speaker*, the *message*, and the *audience*, within a (cultural and historical) *context*. (More specifically, he taught that persuasion occurs from the interaction of the *ethos* of the speaker, the *logos* of the message, and the *pathos* of the audience.) While writers since Aristotle have often used other terms for the speaker (such as the "communicator" or "source") and for the audience (such as the "receiver" or "receptor"), Aristotle's essential model has served as the prevailing model of the communication process for twenty-three centuries.

Much of the unusual communicative power of the Celtic Christian movement was attributable to the *ethos* of its communicators and its communities. Aristotle believed that when auditors hear an advocate speaking, they are asking (perhaps subconsciously) whether the speaker can be trusted and believed. Aristotle observed that, in complex matters—like statecraft and religion—in which even the community of specialists cannot agree on what is true, the nonspecialist public accepts "probability." The public accepts the idea, case, or cause that seems most probably true, and their judgment of the idea is influenced by their judgment of the speaker; the advocate they perceive as most trustworthy and believable is probably communicating truth. Aristotle's chief point is memorably expressed in the words of Ralph Waldo Emerson. Emerson defined eloquence as "the art of speaking what you mean and are," and he suggested that "the reason why anyone refuses his assent to your opinion, or his aid to your benevolent design, is in you. He refuses to accept you as a bringer of truth, because, though you think you have it, he feels that you have it not. You have not given him the authentic sign."[3]

Let's revisit someone in whom the Irish perceived "the authentic sign." Following his Macedonian call, Patrick must have reentered Ireland with the most remarkable *ethos* of any missionary who ever undertook a frontier mission. We can easily imagine the rumor that would have spread like wildfire across the Irish grapevines: "Our slave Patrick has returned, at great personal risk, loving us and saying that the High God loves us." Many stories circulated that reflected his compassion and his understanding of the Irish, such as the following: "They brought him a sick woman who was with child. He baptized the son in the mother's womb, the amniotic fluid being the water of baptism. They buried her below the bank of the church enclosure."[4]

One critical incident suggests the contagion of the grapevine rumors about Patrick, and the electric *ethos* that his courageous return to Ireland had triggered. Patrick resolved, early in his mission, to return to the region where he lived as a slave. Patrick wanted to pay the bond money for his ransom to the druid Miliuc, now an old man, who had bought him from the slave traders; and he wanted to tell him about Christ who paid the ransom for Miliuc's freedom from sin and death. When Miliuc heard that Patrick was en route to see him, he locked himself inside his house and burned it down.[5]

Despite Patrick's high ethos, which undoubtedly assured Patrick a hearing in many tribes, he never "had it made" in his mission to Ireland. The high regard in which many Irish people held him posed a threat to many druids and some tribal kings, who opposed him, often with threats. His published "Declaration" mentions imprisonment, reenslavement, and "the twelve dangers which threatened [his] life."[6] Often, he had to pay for "protection" as he traveled. Yet the apostle's willingness to endure continuing danger for his mission would have fueled "the authentic sign."

What is involved in "the authentic sign" for which audiences are attuned? What, specifically, are people looking for? Aristotle identified three principles in the communicator's ethos: *intelligence*, *character*, and *good will*. To be believed, the speaker must be perceived to be informed, knowledgeable, and competent in the subject matter, with a capacity for valid reasoning, good judgment, and wisdom. To be trusted, the speaker must be perceived as a person of honesty, virtue, and integrity. To be believed and trusted, the speaker needs to be perceived as "for" the audience, on their side, more concerned for the audience's welfare than for self gain. The communicator's ethos is so crucial that Aristotle claimed it is "almost . . . the controlling factor in persuasion."[7]

Later research has uncovered some additional components of ethos that are operative for many auditors, if not all. For example, Aristotle focused on "intrinsic" ethos; that is, the audience's appraisal of the speaker during the speech. Since Aristotle, many writers have demonstrated that "extrinsic" ethos; that is, the speaker's reputation (and perhaps his or her organization's reputation) prior to the speech is also a factor. Patrick, for example, rode a wave of high (extrinsic) ethos as he entered each settlement, but his demeanor, speaking, and life with each settlement of people would have established their high (intrinsic) perception of him.

Again, we now know that some auditors need to experience a speaker's *dynamism;* they have to receive "energy" from the communicator to maintain their interest. If the speaker exudes energy, this seems to amplify the auditor's (positive or negative) perception of the speaker's intelligence, character, and motivation.[8]

Helmut Thielicke, a renowned German theologian and preacher, identified *credibility* as an operative factor in a communicator's ethos.[9] We live, he maintained, in an age of "paid propagandists" for causes ranging from consumer products to political candidates. In that context, hearers want to know whether this politician will deliver on his promises if elected. They want to know if that sports star really uses the underarm deodorant he advertises, and whether it really transformed his social life, or whether he is just a paid propagandist for a large corporation. Thielicke observed, in twentieth-century Germany, that secular audiences were asking credibility-related questions about advocates for Christianity. Do Christian speakers live by this religion they are asking us to buy, or are they just paid propagandists for the institutional church?

My interview research with secular people has confirmed the prominence of the "credibility" theme in secular people's inquiries about Christianity, and their inquiries often take one of three specific forms. First, some people wonder whether we really believe what we say we believe. Second, some people do not doubt that we believe it; they wonder whether we live by it. Third, some people do not doubt that we believe it or live by it; they wonder whether it makes much difference!

The final factor related to ethos is *identification;* this factor relates to the communicator's ethos and also to a kind of relationship between the communicator and the receptors. The concept of identification has had two prominent champions: Søren Kierkegaard and Kenneth Burke. Identification is the deepest and most complex of our concepts related to the communicator's ethos; Kierkegaard and Burke each wrote several volumes devoted (in part) to this concept.

At its heart however, identification refers to a closeness that the audience experiences between themselves and the communicator. If, in the Good Will dimension, auditors ask "Is the communicator *for* us?" then in the Identification dimension they ask "Is the communicator *with* us?" We limit our exploration of this idea to the insights from Kierkegaard and Burke that are reflected in what we know about communication within the spread of Celtic Christianity.

Burke, a twentieth-century Marxist rhetorical theorist, prefers the term "identification" to "persuasion" in his study of the rhetoric of human influence, because identification suggests that the factors in public influence are partially unconscious. The communicator's purpose is to establish rapport, bonding, even community with the receptors; influence comes through such shared images, feelings, attitudes, beliefs, values, and experiences that the communicator and people experience "consubstantiality."[10]

How does Burke's communicator build such rapport? Essentially, communicators achieve identification by understanding, adapting to, and identifying with their audiences. More specifically, communicators do this by identifying with some of the people's beliefs, attitudes, values, needs, issues, and struggles, and by speaking their language and communicating within their thought patterns. Burke proposes using music, visual symbols, and the context to facilitate the experience of community. The speaker should involve the auditor in active thought, or in anticipating what comes next. Mobilizing the people into group participation, like laughter or hand clapping, can build community.

Kierkegaard, the eighteenth-century Danish existentialist philosopher and theologian, also believed that identification is the means through which advocates influence people. He specifically addressed the "Christendom" problem—in which many people who live in a "Christian country" believe in Christianity but do not live by it and do not see the contradiction, and they live with the "illusion" that they are Christians! A "direct" approach to such people, Kierkegaard observed, arouses defensiveness and is counterproductive. So he recommended "indirect" communication approaches that engage people's imaginations, such as through narrative, that "wound from behind" and help people to "discover" truth. He exclaims:

The method must be indirect. . . . All the old military science, all the apologetic and whatever goes with it, serves rather—candidly speaking—to betray the cause of Christianity. At every instant and at every point the tactics must be adapted to a fight which is waged against a conceit, an illusion.[11]

Some of Kierkegaard's strategies—such us employing an "ambiguity" in speech that requires people in denial to think—are more appropriate to his Christendom context (in which the people know enough about Christianity to inform their thinking) than to either the pre-Christian contexts that the Celtic Christian movement usually faced, or the post-Christian contexts we face increasingly in the West. In pre-Christian and post-Christian contexts, the advocate cannot assume basic Christian knowledge in the minds of the audience, so clarity is an absolute requirement for engaging most of the people. Nevertheless, storytelling and other appeals to the imagination are effective with many pre-Christian and post-Christian populations, and a sole reliance on direct propositional speaking is seldom as effective as it *should be* anywhere.

The following suggestions from Kierkegaard should be useful in most apostolic settings. First, engage and speak as though personally, to individuals, not as to an audience *en masse.* As William Warren Sweet once observed, "To personalize religion is to emotionalize it."[12] Second, speak concretely, even poetically and imaginatively, rather than in abstractions. Third, speak to yourself as well as to the auditors, so that the speech has the effect of the audience overhearing the speaker addressing the speaker. Fourth, stress possibility; that is, what a person's life can become. If you tell stories of heroes of the faith, the goal is not for the people to admire the heroes (that is counterproductive) but to glimpse what their own lives can become. Fifth, reject all temptation to pressure people to decide now; respect their freedom and encourage their free response in measurable time.

We can infer that Patrick spoke with sufficient dynamism to engage the Celtic people who were used to eloquent speakers and splendid storytellers; Patrick's results suggest that he competed effectively with their indigenous communicators. We know more than enough to be satisfied that his perceived intelligence, character, good will, and credibility contributed to his evangelization of thirty or more tribes.

Only with time did the extent to which Patrick identified with the Irish, and with his converts and churches, become obvious to the British Church leaders back home, and perhaps to himself. However, by the later years of his twenty-eight-year ministry in Ireland, when he wrote his "Declaration" and his "Letter," Patrick had identified completely with the Irish. Thomas Cahill observes that

> His love for his adopted people shines through his writings, and it is not just a generalized "Christian" benevolence, but a love for individuals as they are. . . . He worries constantly for his people, not just for their spiritual but for their physical welfare. . . . Patrick has become an Irishman.[13]

Patrick's "Letter Against the Soldiers of Coroticus"[14] is written to British "Christian" soldiers who have denied both the Christian identity and the real humanity of the Irish Christians that they kidnapped and sold into slavery. In the letter, Patrick denounces the British slave traders as "dogs" and "fellow-citizens of the demons," he uses his episcopal authority to excommunicate them from the Church, and he leaves no doubt about who are now his people. "He is no longer British or Roman, at all. When he cries out in his pain, 'Is it a shameful thing . . . that we have been born in Ireland?' We know that he has left the old civilization behind forever and has identified himself completely with the Irish."[15] So, from the case of Patrick of Ireland, we can appreciate Aristotle's musing that, among the three modes of persuasion—*ethos, logos,* and *pathos*—ethos is "almost . . . the controlling factor in persuasion."

In the generations after Patrick, the continued spread of Celtic Christianity is substantially attributable to the ethos of the Celtic Christian leaders (and their communities). Unfortunately, the ancient biographers who were most devoted to perpetuating the memories of the Celtic saints are the least useful for helping us understand today how their Ethos fueled the spread of Christianity. In the early medieval western world, most writers of the lives of saints felt obligated to demonstrate that their hero was a Saint—by the extravagant standards of the times. Two examples will show this.

Muirchu's *Life of St. Patrick* is a memorable celebration of the life and ministry of Patrick which incorporates stories from early sources such as Patrick's "Declaration" and Tirechan's *Account* along with other material.[16] Some of this material reflects our theme. A pagan swineherder named Dichu, for instance, misperceived Patrick and his party for robbers as they approached, and Dichu resolved to kill them: "but when he saw the face of St. Patrick the Lord changed his mind for the better, and Patrick preached the faith to him."[17]

Though Patrick's own writing had reported new births, new churches, and changed lives, he had not featured extraordinary miracles from his ministry; Muirchu does feature miracles, however, because he believes that "the Lord . . . confirmed [Patrick's] words by the miracles that followed"[18] In one incident, a druid who opposed Patrick was raised into the air; when he fell, "he smashed his skull on a rock, and died right before them, and the heathen were afraid." The king became enraged and sent his army against Patrick, but a sudden earthquake destroyed many of the king's chariots, horses, and warriors. As the king and his remaining warriors still pursued Patrick, Patrick and his band disappeared before the king's eyes, and the king saw only deer before him.[19] In several accounts of Patrick's confrontations with druids, Patrick causes liquid in a glass to freeze, snow to disappear, fields are made barren, and druid opponents are struck dead. Following Patrick's death, his body mysteriously disappears—by Muirchu's embellished account.

The *Life of St. Columba* by Adamnan of Iona[20] is like Muirchu's *Life of St. Patrick,* only more so. Virtually the entire burden of Adamnan's story is to establish Columba's sainthood in terms of three expectations. Adamnan believed that he had to demonstrate that Columba experienced many prophetic revelations (book one), that he was the agent of many divine miracles (book two), and that "angelic apparitions and certain phenomena of heavenly light [were] seen above the man of God (book three)."[21] As Adamnan tells stories that substantiate these three claims, we can obviously infer insights about the saint's dynamism, character, good will, credibility, and even his compassionate identification with the Picts to whom he and his people were sent. Yet on one rare occasion when Adamnan reports a slice of Columba's apostolic ministry to the Picts, he reports the conversion and baptizing of a Pictish household as a prologue to telling us that Columba raised one of the family's children from death. "At the saint's glorious word the soul returned to the body, and the boy that was dead opened his eyes and lived again."[22] So the literary champions of the Celtic apostles can teach us something about their ethos, if we can distinguish insight from legend. We may learn more, however, from a writer who kept some distance from the Celtic Christian leaders. One such source stands out.

The Venerable Bede was a persistent, even obsessional, champion of the Roman approach to Christianity vis-à-vis the Celtic approach and, as we have seen, all other cultural approaches. So he substantially disagreed with, and criticized, the Celtic Christian leaders who celebrated Easter on the wrong Sunday and wore their hair wrong and did church in a hundred ways that were not culturally Roman. In regard to one factor in ethos theory, Bede took a somewhat low view of the intelligence of the Celtic Christian leaders. Their "zeal for God," as in celebrating Easter on the "wrong" Sunday, was "not entirely according to knowledge."[23] Yet Bede recognized the orthodox theology of the Celtic Christian leaders, and he was profoundly impressed, and moved, by the character and credibility of the Celtic saints, and by their empathy for the populations they reached. For example, Bede reports on the achievement of Columba and his people in establishing Iona, multiplying monasteries, and reaching the Picts of Scotland:

> Columba turned them to the faith of Christ by his words and example. . . . He left successors distinguished for their great abstinence, their love of God, and their observance of the Rule. It is true that they used tables of doubtful accuracy in fixing the date of . . . Easter; but they diligently practiced such works of religion and chastity as they were able to learn from the words of the prophets, the evangelists, and the apostles.[24]

Bede describes at greater length the character, credibility, and incarnational ministry of Aidan, apostle to the Anglo-Saxons of northern England. While still in Iona, before he was sent to establish Lindisfarne to reach the English,

> Aidan taught the clergy many lessons about the conduct of their lives but above all he left them a most salutary example of abstinence and self-control; and the best recommendation of his teaching to all was that he taught them no other way of life than that which he himself practiced among his fellows. For he neither sought after nor cared for worldly possessions but he rejoiced to hand over at once, to any poor man he met, the gifts which he had received from kings or rich men of the world. He used to travel every-

where, in town and country, not on horseback but on foot, unless compelled by urgent necessity to do otherwise, in order that, as he walked along, whenever he saw people whether rich or poor, he might at once approach them [in behalf of the Christian faith].

I have written these things about the character and work of Aidan, not by any means commending or praising his lack of knowledge in the matter of the observance of Easter; indeed, I heartily detest it, . . . but, as a truthful historian, . . . praising . . . his qualities.[25]

Bede continues to commend Aidan for his love of peace, for his "charity" and a dozen other virtues, and for "his soul which triumphed over anger and greed . . . . But . . . he did not observe Easter at the proper time!"[26] Bede also affirmed the ethos of St. Cuthbert, a successor to Aidan in leading Celtic Christian expansion in England. While he sees much the same character and credibility in Cuthbert he saw in Columba and Aidan, he was especially impressed by Cuthbert's identification with the most marginalized unreached people of Anglo-Saxon society:

Now he used especially to make for those places and preach in those villages that were far away on steep and rugged mountains, which others dreaded to visit and whose poverty and ignorance kept other teachers away. Giving himself up gladly to this devoted labour, he attended to their instruction with such industry that he would leave the monastery and often not return home for a whole week, sometimes even for two or three weeks and even occasionally for a whole month; but he would linger among the hill folk, calling the peasants to heavenly things both by the words he said and by his virtuous deeds.[27]

Bede also held a positive image of the several Celtic monastic communities that he knew something about. For instance, he commended the credibility of the large community of men and women at Whitby, founded and led by St. Hilda: "After the example of the primitive church, no one was rich, no one was in need, for they had all things in common and none had any private property."[28]

However, our assurance of the character, good will, and credibility of these communities depends much less upon the observations of historians than upon the "circumstantial evidence" from what they achieved and how. They reached one "barbarian" population after another by welcoming seekers, who were looking for "the authentic sign," into the close fellowship of their monastic communities, where seekers closely observed how the Christians lived, day after day. As seekers spent time with a Celtic Christian community, they typically found themselves believing what the Christians taught. Indeed, the Celtic Christians undoubtedly discovered that the presence of seekers observing them for "the authentic sign" provided an additional incentive for living faithful lives.

Aristotle observed that people are much more likely to respond to a message if, in addition to understanding it, they experience the emotion that energizes an appropriate response. Information and reasons alone are unlikely to trigger action. Thomas De Quincey, standing in Aristotle's tradition, compared a speech to a ship; to move the ship (the audience) you need both a rudder (understanding) and a sail (passion).[29] Aristotle taught that we arouse human emotions in other people indirectly—by describing the object, person, or situation that, when seen in their imaginations, stimulates the desired emotion. Much later, George Campbell was to connect emotions to motives and desires; when people see the possibility that some deep desire can be fulfilled (or frustrated), they respond emotionally. A third way that a communicator might arouse emotions is through the use of emotionally loaded language, but if the communicator is not granted high ethos, that tactic can backfire.

The Irish and the other Celtic peoples (but especially the Irish) were passionate people who experienced the full range of human emotions and usually based decisions on how they felt. We have already seen that the Romans viewed the Celtic emotional intensity and volatility as one sign they were "barbarians." This image has stuck over time. In the nineteenth century, England's prime minister Benjamin Disraeli characterized the Irish as a "wild, reckless, indolent, uncertain and superstitious race."[30] Thomas Cahill explains what drove the Irish emotional agenda:

> Fixity escaped these people, as in the end it escapes us all. They understood, as few have understood before or since, how fleeting life is and how pointless to try to hold on to things or people. They pursued the wondrous deed, the heroic gesture: fighting, fucking, drinking, art—poetry for intense emotion, the music that accompanied the heroic drinking with which each day ended . . . . All these are worth pursuit, and the first, especially, will bring the honor great souls seek. But in the midst of this furious swirl of energy lies a still point of detachment. . . . The face of the *Dying Gaul* speaks for them all: each one of us will die, naked and alone, on some battlefield not of our own choosing. . . . After the assassination of John F. Kennedy, Daniel Patrick Moynihan was heard to say that to be Irish is to know that in the end the world will break your heart.[31]

We do not know precisely how the apostles to the Celts engaged in emotional appeals, because we have no transcripts, or even elaborate summaries, of their discourse to the pagans. We can infer four insights. First, apostles like Patrick "had to find a way of connecting his message to their deepest concerns."[32] You cannot engage people without engaging their motivational and emotional agenda. Second, in contrast to the indifference of their capricious gods, the people discovered that their feelings mattered to the Triune God of Christianity. Third, their experience of God's Providence gave them victory over terror and other destructive emotions. Fourth, Christianity gave them outlets for expressing their constructive emotions through indigenous oratory, storytelling, poetry, music, dance, drama, etc. in God's service. So, the Celtic Christian movement was effective, in part, because its leaders took the *pathos* of the Celtic audience seriously.

We have seen that much of the communicative power of the Celtic Christian movement was attributable to the *ethos* of its communicators, who affirmed and engaged the *pathos* of the Celtic audience. Turning now to the *logos* of the message, we see that while Patrick, Columba, Aidan, and the others could reason quite effectively with people, their genius (compared to the Romans) was in the *imaginative* communication of Christianity's message.

Several specific communication strategies (anticipated in the material from Burke and Kierkegaard, above) help account for the communicative effectiveness of their movement as well. Each of these communication strategies represents one way to express the larger principle of Imagination. Celtic Christianity took an imaginative approach to communicating the gospel mystery to "barbarians." They tapped their own imaginations for fresh ways to communicate the good news, and they engaged the imaginations of pre-Christian seekers. Thomas Cahill tells us that "Patrick found a way of swimming down to the depths of the Irish psyche and warming and transforming Irish imagination—making it more humane and more noble while keeping it Irish.[33]

Over two centuries ago, a Scottish rhetorician named George Campbell elevated imagination to a prominent place in our understanding of the communication process, and subsequent history (as well as our study of prior history) has confirmed his judgment. In Campbell's theory, "to please the imagination" became one of the four possible goals of a speech,[34] and engaging people's imaginations is often a means of achieving any of the other three goals of speech—"to enlighten the understanding," "to move the passions," and "to influence the will." Campbell, writing in 1776, adhered to the informal "Faculty Psychology" school of thought instituted by Francis Bacon. Faculty Psychologists believed that the human brain essentially functions in five ways—reasoning, feeling, imagining, remembering, and willing, and that these five "faculties" were rooted in distinct parts of the brain.

More recent research in brain anatomy has undermined Campbell's model, but the faculty psychologists nevertheless anticipated a model that now features the two "hemispheres" of the cerebrum. This model suggests that the left hemisphere controls the right side of the body and mental functions like speech, while the right hemisphere controls the left side of the body and mental functions like the perception of spatial relationships. Some people are predominantly "left-brained" analytical, and some people are predominantly "right-brained" artistic. Furthermore, some cultures are predominantly left-brained, and some are predominantly right-brained, and cultures can shift in their predominant orientation over time. In this theory, logical thinking, conceptualizing, and verbalizing are left-brained, "rational" activities, while intuiting, feeling, and imagining are right-brained, "experiential" activities. The following chart suggests some of the distinctions:[35]

Left Brain	Right Brain
logic	intuition
concepts	emotions
abstraction	imagination
language	art, music, poetry
rational	experience

Some mental activities, like remembering and willing, are undoubtedly rooted in both hemispheres of the brain.

The Irish and other Celtic peoples were predominantly right-brained and, in reaching them, Christianity adapted remarkably from its earlier Roman reliance upon words, propositions, concepts, and theological abstractions. Ian Bradley reports that Celtic Christianity was rooted more in the imagination than the intellect, and spoke in images more than in concepts. Celtic Christian leaders

> excelled at expressing their faith in symbols, metaphors and images, both visual and poetic. They had the ability to . . . paint pictures in words, signs and music that acted as icons opening windows on heaven and pathways to eternity. . . . They have much to teach Christians today seeking to rekindle their imaginative faculties.[36]

Celtic Christian communicators spoke from their imaginations to the imaginations of their hearers. They were less interested than the Church's Roman wing in "apologetics"; that is, rationally proving the validity of Christianity's truth claims; they seem to have believed that if you could make a Christian truth claim clear to the people's imaginations, the people and the Holy Spirit would take it from there. So *analogies* were widely used, as in the tradition's belief that St. Patrick used the small shamrock plant to show how God could be both three and one. The Celtic Christian movement especially relied on *poetry* to engage the people's imaginations. One ancient poem, attributed to St. David, exclaims that

> No man is the son of knowledge if he is not also the son of
>   poetry.
> No man loves poetry without loving the light,
> Nor the light without loving the truth,
> Nor the truth without loving justice,
> Nor justice without loving God.[37]

The Celtic communication of Christian truth was known to combine genres, like analogy and poetry, as in this early Irish verse:

Three folds of the cloth, yet only one napkin is there,
Three joints in the finger, but still only one finger fair;
Three leaves of the shamrock, yet no more than one
    shamrock to wear,
Frost, snow-flakes and ice, all in water their origin share,
Three Persons in God; to one God alone we make prayer.[38]

Celtic Christian advocates especially engaged barbarian imaginations through *storytelling* and *poetry*. The several Celtic peoples revered their oral traditions; their bards told stories and their poets recited poems that communicated the people's beliefs, history, and folk wisdom through entertainment. Their "poets constituted the intellectual aristocracy of Celtic society . . . . The Celts regarded poets as . . . intermediaries between this world and the next," and their storytelling bards were also greatly esteemed. "To a considerable extent, . . . Christian monks and scholars took over the role of the old Druidic bards and *filid*."[39] Many of them became prodigious storytellers. They communicated much of the biblical message by telling its stories, and many of their more original stories, and the stories of the saints, were passed to many generations through the oral tradition.

"Celtic Music" is enormously popular once again, so we are not surprised to learn that Christianity engaged the Celtic peoples, and other "barbarians," through their *music*. The Celtic peoples were as musically oriented as any people of history. Ian Bradley reports that "the Celts sang as they worked, as they played and as they prayed."[40] Celtic music's distinctive repetitive and rhythmic qualities proved useful to the Christian revelation, and useful to developing devout souls and communities.

Vincent Donovan, the modern Catholic apostle to the Masai people of East Africa, once observed that Protestant Christian leaders seem to trust only the sense of hearing, and therefore rely almost totally upon using the preached and taught Word to reach and teach people. By contrast, he said, Celtic Catholics believe that God can use all five senses to "speak" to people.

Celtic Christianity strongly illustrates this through its use of the *visual arts*. For instance, they used the famous "Celtic Knot," whose spirals intertwine endlessly to symbolize God's encircling protection of his people, to symbolize eternity, and to suggest the movement, pilgrimage and progress that is essential in the Christian's life.[41] Again, Celtic Christianity's distinctive tall standing cross, with a circle intersecting the upper half of the cross, was an imaginative way to visually integrate the themes of creation and redemption.[42] The biblical scenes sometimes carved at the base of a cross served as teaching aids. The theme of *imagination* thus helps us to see that the Celtic Christian movement took an intentionally "redundant" approach to communicating Christianity. They did not rely, as some traditions come close to, upon preaching alone to communicate the fullness of Christianity. They seem to have employed as many different "media" as they could to get the message across, and to get people involved with the message.

As we have already seen, Kierkegaard declared that one way to achieve identification with a people is to stress possibility; that is, what the people's lives can become. Helping the Irish to imagine what they could become may have been Patrick's most profound rhetorical achievement, all the more notable when we contrast Patrick with his near-contemporary, Augustine. Thomas Cahill suggests that

> Patrick's emotional grasp of Christian truth may have been greater than Augustine's. Augustine looked into his own

heart and found there the inexpressible anguish of each individual, which enabled him to articulate a theory of sin that has no equal—the dark side of Christianity. Patrick prayed, made peace with God, and then looked not only into his own heart but into the hearts of others. What he saw convinced him of the bright side—that even slave traders can turn into liberators, even murderers can act as peacemakers, even barbarians can take their place among the nobility of heaven.[43]

CHAPTER 6

The Missionary Perspective of Celtic Christianity

t one level, the Celtic Christian leaders and people were a simple study. Their lives, and communities, were open books. In stark contrast to the secretive religion of the druids, the monastic communities and the churches they planted were open to everyone, with no secrets from anyone. They never claimed to be other than they were, or more than they were. They were devoted, compassionate, sold-out citizens of Heaven. They relied, through "prayer without ceasing," upon the Triune God's providence and power. They would do anything they could to help other people find The Way.

At another level, however, the Celtic Christian movement functioned with such intuitive sophistication that, in the academic field of "Missiology," we have only recently learned enough to name and describe some of what they knew, and did, that contributed to their reach and growth.

We have already explored some of these themes. We saw that the contagion of their movement was partly attributable to the formation of their people, in the monastic communities, for ministry and witness. We observed their mission band approach to planting churches in settlements, and their faith that focused on people's "middle" daily issues as well as the ultimate religious issues. We saw how their *ethos*, their identification with the people, their emotional appeal, and their imaginal appeal all helped communicate the gospel. We saw how their strategy of indigenizing the forms for expressing Christianity in the life and culture of each "barbarian" population helped the gospel's meaning to break through time and again. By the eleventh century their "culturally relevant" movement had adapted Christianity to the language and culture of many different Celtic and Germanic peoples; indeed, the number of cultural adaptations they managed was unprecedented. We saw that they consistently paid the price to understand the target language and culture, although there were exceptions. Columba, we think, never really learned a Pictish language, so his occasional missions in Scotland employed an interpreter.[1] That is why, presumably, he personally did more evangelism in his first career in Ireland than after he left for Iona "to convert the Picts." Nevertheless, he was a marvelous mission executive in Scotland, and many of his people mastered Pictish culture and languages.

We have not yet reflected upon the way in which, as part of their "indigenization" strategy, the pioneers of Celtic Christianity "contextualized" Christianity's message for the several Celtic peoples. The Biblical Revelation was primary, but understanding the people's cultural and historical context helped them to know what in Scripture to feature first and how to "translate" it for the people. This principle is crucial because, as David Bosch observes, "The Christian faith never exists except as 'translated' into a culture."[2]

We can see the importance of the indigenization (or translation) principle through what may be a negative example in the history of the evangelization of the Picts. Most historians, following Bede, tell us that St. Columba's people evangelized the Picts of northern Scotland; it was not necessary to reach the Picts of southern Scotland, because "St. Ninian" had already reached them. We know very little about Ninian; most of what we do know comes from these lines in Bede's _Ecclesiastical History_:

Columba . . . came to Britain to preach the word of God to the kingdoms of the northern Picts which are separated from the southern part of their land by steep and rugged mountains. The southern Picts who live on this side of the mountains had, so it is said, long ago given up the errors of idolatry and received the true faith through the preaching of the Word by that reverend and holy man Bishop Ninian, a Briton who had received orthodox instruction at Rome in the faith and the mysteries of the truth. His episcopal see is celebrated for its church, . . . [which] is commonly called Whithorn, the White House, because Ninian built a church of stone there, using a method unusual among the Britons.[3]

In a departure from his usual attention to detail, Bede tells us nothing about how Ninian and his people went about their mission, nor does he give dates for Ninian's ministry. Nora Chadwick reports that the traditional date for Ninian's founding of Whithorn is A.D. 397, and that he died around A.D. 432,[4] which would place his work in the early fifth century.

Now, one early source indicates that Ninian's work among the Southern Picts did not last. By the time Patrick wrote his "Letter Against the Soldiers of Coroticus," (perhaps in the mid-450s A.D.) he refers twice to the Southern Picts as "apostate," i. e. no longer faithful to the Christian religion.[5] This is not, for Patrick, a mere rumor or an incidental allusion but a centerpiece in his slavery drama; Coroticus' Briton soldiers have sold Patrick's Irish converts to the "vilest, worthless, apostate Picts."[6] Louis Gougaud also concluded that "the Southern Picts converted by Ninian did not persevere in the faith"; Columba's people, he suggests, had to reach the Southern Picts again, as well as reach the Northern Picts for the first time.[7]

We lack adequate knowledge of who Ninian and his people really reached from their base at Whithorn. Indeed, Hume Brown suggests that "who these Picts were and what is implied in this vague notion of their conversion will probably never be determined; and, as a matter of fact, all traces of Ninian's labours disappear during the centuries that followed the withdrawal of the [Roman] legion."[8]

Two possibilities are suggested by the slender evidence. First, Ninian's mission may have confined its outreach to the Southern Picts who had adopted Latin and Roman culture during the Roman occupation. Second, they may have reached Picts who had not been substantially Romanized, but with culturally Roman Christianity. In either case, the churches that Ninian's mission planted were quite small, and they marched to the Roman drum. At the Whithorn headquarters, the church was built out of stone (as the Romans would do), rather than from the planks and wattle that were used in culturally Celtic architecture. Bede strongly sponsors Ninian's *curriculum vitae*: Ninian "had received orthodox instruction at Rome in the faith and the mysteries of the truth." We already know what that meant for the Roman wing of the church, and for Bede. It meant, as David Bosch reminds us, "that a 'missionary church' must reflect in every detail the Roman custom of the moment."[9] The cemeteries that have survived are all Roman.

Why did the Southern Picts fall away? It is possible, of course, that the first generation of Southern Pict Christians understood the Christian message and ethic and became real Christians, but the second or third generation simply lapsed into nominality or paganism. That has happened in other young churches; indeed, every church struggles with the challenge of passing on the meaning of the faith to each succeeding generation. If Ninian planted small churches, and only in Romanized Pict communities, the movement probably lacked the critical mass necessary for long term survival. If Ninian reached non-Romanized Picts with

Roman Christianity, they may have never really understood the Christianity they received from Ninian and his people—as presented in Latin language and Roman forms. More likely, however, the Southern Picts understood enough from Roman Christianity to know, say, that they wanted to go to heaven, and they learned the Roman rituals enough to go through the motions—but without understanding enough Christian meaning to pass it on, in their own ways, to their children. That has happened in many other cases of mission, both Roman and Protestant; when the missionaries imposed Western forms, the people learned the foreign forms but did not understand the meaning. As Bosch reminds us, "the Christian faith never exists except as 'translated' into a culture!"

In contrast to Ninian and Bede, and the whole Roman wing of the Church, Celtic Christian leaders understood the indigenizing principle, and the need for the principle, and they developed some sophistication in selectively applying the principle. For example, they understood that the Christian movement should always employ the people's language. They probably observed that using indigenous music is usually most effective, but some "foreign" music will catch on. In the communication of Christianity's essential message, they undoubtedly discovered that many of the "transcultural" teachings and stories of the Scriptures were easily communicated in the tribal cultures of Britain and Europe, but some additional "contextualization" is always useful. Three examples will demonstrate this insight.

The first example focuses on the doctrine of the Trinity, and demonstrates that, in the specific context, some opportunities to contextualize should be obvious to any Christian communicator who studies the target culture.

Patrick would have observed several traits in the Irish

Celts that, together, suggested one communicative response. The Irish, perhaps from the teachings of the druids or the primal religion that preceded the druids, were aware that Ultimate Reality was mysterious and complex, and they were comfortable with paradox; nevertheless, they had "a bureaucrat's love of classification."[10] Brendan Lehane reports that the Irish also believed that some numbers were significant; the number three was especially powerful, and their characteristic way of structuring thought about complex matters was

> the triad, an arrangement of three statements which summed up a thing or person or quality or mood, or simply linked otherwise incompatible things. Three false sisters were said to be 'perhaps', 'maybe' and 'I dare say': three timid brothers 'Hush', 'Stop', and 'Listen'. The three keys that unlock thoughts were drunkenness, trustfulness, love. . . . If there were paradox or pun in a triad, so much the better. . . . The Irish had their liking for riddles too. . . . Everyone was thought to be spiritually tied to three . . . lumps of earth, the three sods of fate. The first was that on which he was born, the sod of birth. Second was that on which he died. And the third marked the place of his burial.[11]

The Irish Celts even imagined some of their gods and (especially) goddesses in groups of threes, and one god was believed to have three faces! Now, given such knowledge of the people, most missionaries would readily perceive that the Irish people had been "shaped" by history, by culture, and by preparatory grace to appreciate a Trinitarian explanation of God. So, when Irish seekers ask Patrick how Christianity understands God, he withdraws, from the bank of Christian doctrine, the doctrine of the Trinity.

> Our God is the God of all people, the God of heaven and earth. . . . His life is in all things; he makes all things live; he governs all things; he supports all things . . . He has a son

who is coeternal with him and of like nature . . . and the Holy Spirit breathes in them. The Father, the Son and the Holy Spirit are not separate.[12]

The doctrine of the Trinity became the foundational paradigm for Celtic Christianity. The doctrine informed the people's piety as well as the theologians' theories. The understanding of God as a unity of three persons, bound together in love, became the Celtic model for the Christian community; the understanding of God as a family of three persons defined the Christian family. Celtic Christians lived their daily lives, from waking up to cleaning up, from working to retiring, aware of the presence, protection, and guidance of all three persons of the Trinity.

Their understanding of the doctrine was like the Roman understanding, with two exceptions: First, the Romans emphasized the oneness, or unity, of the Trinity more than the Celts. Second, the Roman Christians emphasized the "transcendence" of the Triune God (later expressed visibly in their Gothic cathedrals), and they seem to have experienced God as distant, if not remote, except for Christ's "real presence" in the sacraments. The Celtic Christians emphasized the "immanence" of the Triune God as Companion in this life and the next; in their experience, the "veil" between earth and heaven was "thin"—if you viewed creation as sacramental. Many centuries after Patrick and Columba, Celtic Christians in the Hebrides Islands prepared for evening prayer with this affirmation:

> I lie down this night with God,
>   And God will lie down with me;
> I lie down this night with Christ,
>   And Christ will lie down with me;
> I lie down this night with the Spirit,
>   And the Spirit will lie down with me;

God and Christ and the Spirit
Be lying down with me.[13]

The second example focuses on a contextually appropriate way to interpret the death of Christ. Thomas Cahill tells us that the Irish were still practicing human sacrifice when Patrick returned. They sacrificed some prisoners of war to appease the war gods, and some of their own newborns to appease the harvest gods, and occasionally a prince would offer himself as a sacrifice to some god whose help was needed.

Three principles drove this sacrificial tradition. First, there were always devoted religious people who were willing to give up their lives to the gods for the people. Second, there were always "basely religious"[14] people who were willing to sacrifice other people to the gods! Third, "It would be an understatement to assert that the Irish gods were not the friendliest of figures."[15] Their gods were capricious; they prepared traps for people; and they would only bless people in response to flattery, liturgical manipulation, and sacrifice. That religious worldview produced a precarious sense of life; no Irishman was unfamiliar with the experience of cosmic terror.

Patrick proclaimed the good news of a different kind of God. Christianity's God is not hostile, capricious, or self-seeking; He is for us, he loves people (and his other creatures), and he wills their deliverance from sin and terror into new life. Patrick, drawing from the Philippian Hymn, proclaimed that this God does not want people to feed him through human sacrifices; this God has sacrificed his only Son for us and wants to feed us through the blessed sacrament. No human being needs to be sacrificed ever again. This High God calls us not to die for him, but to live for him and each other.[16]

The third example also focuses upon a contextualized way to interpret the death of Jesus, developed by St. Aidan as he came to understand the history and values of the

Anglo-Saxons of northern England. In A.D. 625, eight years before Iona commissioned Aidan to Northumbria, Canterbury had commissioned Paulinus to the same region. Paulinus, in the tradition of Ninian, must have imported left-brained, culturally Roman Christianity. Bede's account begins by asserting that "the Northumbrian race . . . accepted the word of faith through the preaching of Paulinus." [17] Bede soon admits, however, that the "heathen" were unresponsive to Paulinus's preaching and, indeed, Paulinus had to work "to prevent those who had come with him from lapsing from the faith!"[18] Paulinus did, however, make some progress with King Edwin and his associates, though the king did not immediately accept the faith.

One day a neighboring king sent a messenger to Edwin's court. Inside his scroll was a poisoned dagger. As the messenger charged to stab Edwin, one member of the court, Lilla, was close enough to step across and take the dagger in his own stomach. The dagger passed through Lilla's body and also wounded Edwin, though not fatally. That night Edwin's queen gave birth to a daughter. Following these two experiences, Edwin asked Paulinus to baptize his baby daughter and eleven other members of his household. In time, after more teaching and reflection (and an inviting letter from the pope), "King Edwin, with all the nobles of his race and a vast number of the common people, received the faith and regeneration by holy baptism in . . . 627."[19]

In time, King Edwin was slain, and Paulinus moved on to serve the church at Rochester. One gets the impression, reading Bede's sections on Aidan's ministry from Lindisfarne, that Aidan and his people found the number of common people who were converts, or even preevangelized, to be much less "vast" than Bede's hype of Paulinus's earlier work had suggested.

Nevertheless, Aidan built upon something important

from that history. People told him the story of Lilla, King Edwin's associate, who had taken the poisoned dagger for the king. Aidan perceived that the courage, loyalty, and devotion that were embodied in Lilla's deed represented ultimate values in this people's culture. Indeed, the deed steeled their conviction that there would be no greater honor than to die for the king you serve.

David Adam reports Aidan's rhetorical response. Aidan told them that he and his people also served as the "soldiers" of a King—for whom they were willing to risk wild animals, or hostile armies, or even death until this whole world becomes the Kingdom of their King.

Then Aidan added the punchline. He and other Christian soldiers represent the King who loved his soldiers and people so much that the King laid down his life for them!

In dying, he won a kingdom for his followers. So Christians have a definite purpose for living, to serve Christ and to live for the glory of God in doing his will. They also have a definite reward. Soldiers on earth can only be rewarded if the king is the victor. Life is eternal, people are free, for Christ has won the victory.[20]

Sometimes the mission context serves not only as a theater for adapting the presentation of Christianity; it also serves as a catalyst for recovering something essential and precious within Christianity.[21] The Celtic Christian approach to Nature was a very distinctive feature of Celtic Christianity, and also represented an important Christian recovery. One day, as Patrick and several companions were surveying the land at Armagh where a church would be built.

> They climbed to that hilltop—and they came on a doe with its little fawn lying in the place where is now the northern altar of the church in Armagh. Patrick's companions wished to catch the fawn and kill it; but Patrick refused to

permit this; instead he caught the fawn himself and carried it on his shoulders, and the doe followed him like a gentle loving sheep until he released the fawn on another hillside to the north of Armagh.[22]

The story of St. Patrick and the deer is one of many such stories. Virtually every Celtic saint was noted for his or her great fondness of, and rapport with, animals and birds. Columba's Iona served as a sanctuary for migratory birds, and a hospital for injured birds; his legend tells of a favored horse shedding tears as Columba lay dying. Cuthbert was befriended by two otters as he prayed while standing in the sea. Columbanus had squirrels, wolves, and other wild animals among his friends. The tradition around St. Kevin of Glendalough tells us that a badger brought him a daily salmon to eat, that birds surrounded him in song as he prayed, and that he once experienced a blackbird laying an egg in his open hand as he prayed. Michael Mitton suggests that "the very strong presence of the Spirit of God in such people affected the animals' response to them."[23]

Somewhat later, the life of Francis of Assisi would feature similar stories of rapport with nature's creatures, which was also interpreted as a sign of the Holy Spirit within him. Such love for animals was extraordinary in the Roman Church; it was comparatively ordinary in the Celtic Church. Indeed, scholars surmise that Francis probably "caught" the Celtic Christian love for nature in his visits to Bobbio, the Celtic monastic community near Assisi.

The Roman Church has always celebrated the life of Francis, but the fact that they regard his love for nature's creatures as unusual indicates Roman Christianity's more detached or impersonal approach to nature.[24] We can observe the difference in their preferred settings for worship: The Celts loved to celebrate the gospel in the open air; the Roman branch preferred thick buildings that walled out the sights and sounds from the world. Roman Christianity's detachment from nature, in time, opened the way for Western humanity's domination and exploitation of nature—which Celtic Christians would have regarded as sinful.

How do we account for Celtic Christianity's reverence for nature's creatures? Ian Bradley suggests that the Celtic love for nature sprang from three "roots."[25] First, love for God's creation is Biblical. Genesis declares the goodness and preciousness of God's creation, the Psalms are filled with a sense of creation's wonder, and Jesus taught that the birds and animals, and even the plants, matter to God. Second, from the Druid nature mysticism that preceded Christianity's introduction, the pagan Celts already respected and revered nature; the Christianity that Patrick brought affirmed and "Christianized" their affinity with nature. Third, Celtic Christians lived in natural settings, so their experience informed their love of nature.

To be sure, the Celts' orientation toward nature changed with their Christianization. On the one hand, Christian faith enhanced the Celts' love for nature while also arming them with God's providence as they faced nature's threats. On the other hand, it changed the way they viewed nature as a source for knowing the Divine. They moved from Pantheism, gods in nature, to a Christian Panentheism, the transcendent God, who is revealed in the history of Israel and in Christ and can *also* be known through nature. They now knew that the history recorded in Scripture was God's primary mode of revelation, while Nature was the "second book" of God.[26]

This point is not easy to communicate, but I recall the memorable way that Ted Runyon, of Emory University's Candler School of Theology, once clarified it: "The psalmist did *not* say 'The heavens declare the glory of God and the firmament showeth his handiwork.' The psalmist said 'The heavens declare the glory of *Yahweh* and the firmament

showeth *His* handiwork.'" Celtic Christianity believed that
the natural world was created good and, though the Fall
introduced sin and evil into the natural order, it was still
essentially God's good creation. Celtic Christians also
believed that the "veil" between the natural and the supernatural, and between earth and heaven, was much "thin-
ner"—especially at "holy places"—than the Roman wing
believed. Consequently, nature figures prominently in their
visual Christian symbols. Ian Bradley observes that

> the artwork which the Celts have left us as their most tan-
> gible legacy is full of the exuberant celebration of creation.
> The borders of the illustrations in their illuminated manu-
> scripts are often made up of intertwining patterns of fruit
> and foliage. Beautifully executed drawings of birds and
> animals serve as punctuation marks on the pages of script.
> The distinctive feature of the Celtic Cross is the circle of cre-
> ation, representing the earth and the sun, which surrounds
> and encompasses the cross of redemption.[27]

The Celtic Christian attitude toward nature could teach us
several things today. First, their affirmation of nature stands
as an outstanding example of a Christian mission moving
into a culture and affirming, and building upon, what it can.
Second, they model the fact that a missionary encounter
with another culture can often help us to perceive, and
recover, something precious in the Christian body of truth.
Third, because they understood nature so intimately that
they saw both the wonder and the threat, they would dis-
suade us from the naive New Age romanticism about nature
often surfacing today. Fourth, they would say that our lives
can be deeply enriched by living in covenant with creation
as well as Creator; the birds and animals can bless us. Fifth,
they would remind us of the basic biblical mandate for people to be the "stewards" of creation, that our exploitation of
creation has polluted the earth and introduced an undeni-

able ecological crisis, so they would counsel us to abandon our denial and commit to loving and restoring the earth.

I experience the most dissonance, even discomfort, in considering the Celtic Christian doctrine of Human Nature. Celtic Christianity's belief in the goodness of creation—infected, but not destroyed, by sin and evil, was matched by a belief in an essential goodness of human nature—to which you could appeal in evangelism.

It is important to acknowledge the roots of Celtic Christianity's optimism about human nature. Genesis sees people created in God's image, and Psalm 8 could still affirm that humans are only a little lower than the angels and are crowned with glory and honor. The Druids had believed in free will and the possibility of willing to live a good life—and succeeding. The Greek Fathers of the Eastern Church had believed that sin had not obliterated the image of God in people nor destroyed their capacity to want, and enjoy, fellowship with God. Origen in Egypt and Irenaeus in Gall held similar views. From these influences, and their own reflections from Scripture and mission experience, Ian Bradley tells us that Celtic Christianity viewed "human nature not as being radically tainted by sin and evil, intrinsically corrupt and degenerate, but as imprinted with the image of God, full of potential and opportunity, longing for completion and perfection."[28]

The Roman Church, however, especially under the sway of St. Augustine, had a significantly different view of human nature. St. Augustine, Christianity's greatest and most profound theological giant, had reflected his way into the view that Original Sin had so corrupted human nature, and twisted it into such pride and selfishness, that people were no longer free to will what God wills. Consequently, everything involved in the salvation of people is by the "irresistible" Grace of the Sovereign God; people do not have enough goodness left within them to even cooperate in their salvation nor, once saved, to live a good life without more Grace.

Augustine's high doctrine of Grace, probably coupled with his observation that some people do in fact resist "irresistible" Grace, led him to a logical conclusion: Augustine's doctrine of Double Election; that is, that God has "wired" some people to be receptive to God's grace, but not others. This difference between Roman and Celtic Christianity is very important for evangelization, because the two views lead to quite contrasting understandings of what is essentially involved in Salvation. For Augustine, Jesus Christ saves us by rescuing us from sin and the consequences of the Fall. For the Celtic apostles, Jesus Christ also comes to complete his good creation.[29]

While we are in no position to "settle" the most enduring problem in a theology of human nature, several observations are warranted. First, Celtic Christianity's theological optimism about human nature cannot adequately account for the Holocaust and the other cases of genocide in the twentieth century; Augustine's doctrine of human nature does account for large scale depravity and for much else that has gone terribly wrong in God's human experiment. Second, it is possible to observe, in most people, both sin and goodness. Third, my interviews with converts indicate that, for many people, becoming a Christian involves experiences of being rescued and experiences of being completed. Fourth, the Celtic Christian movement suggests that it is often more effective to begin with people at the point of their goodness, however latent, than to initially engage people as sinners. Fifth, the Celtic doctrine of human nature enabled Celtic Christians to perceive God's possibilities in the "barbarians," and they engaged in mission to these peoples for five centuries. The Roman doctrine, combined with their expectation that a people be sufficiently "civilized" to be reachable, energized much less mission in these same centuries.

The Celtic missionaries, in every case, reached out to a tribe of people who were already influenced by, perhaps devoted to, one or more religious traditions. These were "primal" or "folk" religions; the best known of these religions today is the religion of the Druids.[30] Every missionary today, indeed every Christian who is engaged in the ministry of witness today, engages people who already have a worldview and are already influenced by, perhaps devoted to, one or more religions or philosophies.

The basic ways that the Celtic Christian movement engaged "people who already have a religion" can instruct us today. On one occasion, in "the territory of Corcu Temne," Patrick came to "the well of Findmag." Tirechan reports that "druids honoured the well and made votive offerings in it as if to a god." Once, the people believed, a seer had provided that his bones would be placed under the rock in the well, so "for this reason they worshipped the well as a god." Patrick, with the help of "my God who lives in heaven," lifted the stone. "They found nothing in the well but water alone, and they believed in the high God."[31] Beside the stone, Patrick baptized a man named Cata.

The Celtic Christian leaders were radical Trinitarian Monotheists who, therefore, saw no reason to welcome other gods into the life of Christian communities. Occasionally, they would confront the local god or their leaders—as in Patrick's occasional "power encounter" with the Druids, or as in the case where Columbanus had to "cleanse" an area by chopping down sacred trees that had become idols.

Such encounters, however, were extraordinary. Michael Mitton observes that Celtic Christian leaders relied strongly on the "spiritual gift of discernment," so they "were very sensitive to presences of good and evil in people and places. They therefore sensed what was good in a community and blessed it accordingly, or they sensed evil, in which case they sought to combat it with prayer."[32] The power encounters were infrequent, however, and the settings requiring a "slash and burn" response were even less frequent. Furthermore, "Nowhere do you get the impression of a powerful ecclesiastical force moving in on reluctant individuals."[33]

Generally, a mission team would visit a Celtic settlement, befriend the people, and engage in conversation and some presentation to "make known God's gift and the eternal comfort He provides."[34] In time, they would invite the people to confess faith and form into a church, but there was no manipulation, coercion, or force; they believed Christ wanted people's free response. They affirmed and built on every indigenous feature that they could. They affirmed the Celtic people's religious aspirations, their sense of divinity's closeness, their belief in an afterlife, their love for creation and, as we have seen, their fascination with the number three. Celtic missionaries seem to have believed that God's prevenient grace had preceded them and prepared the people for the gospel. They seem to have believed that, just as Jesus came to the Jews not to destroy the law and the prophets but to fulfill them, so he comes to every people "not to destroy, but to fulfill" their religious tradition.

We can see this policy visually in the evolution of the tall Celtic stone crosses. When Patrick returned to Ireland, the Irish Celts already worshiped around tall "standing stones." The pillars stood as a symbol of the people's desire to reach up to the heavens and the High God; they stood as a symbolic link between heaven and earth. Once, when the people were more nomadic, a tall tree might serve as such a symbol; when they gathered into settlements, the standing stone became the favored symbol.[35] When a people turned to the Christian faith, the people often "Christianized" their standing stone by carving or painting a cross, the sign of the fish, or the Chi-Rho symbol on the stone, and it became a place made sacred for Christian worship. In time, this practice led to the sculpting, from tall stones, of tall standing Celtic crosses with the circle intersecting the cross. In time, biblical scenes and/or nature scenes were carved onto some crosses.

The Celtic Christian movement often built chapels on or near the grove, or the well, or the hill that had served as a sacred site for the primal religion. The sacred site would often retain its former name or a reminiscent name. Celtic Christianity often retained, and "Christianized," some of the prior religion's holy days, festivals, and ceremonies, thereby "grafting" the new onto the old. Christian priests and monks often wore a clothing or hairstyle reminiscent of the people's former priests. Celtic Christianity preferred continuity rather than discontinuity, inclusion rather than exclusion. Celtic Christianity was a fairly "religion-friendly" movement.

It is important to note that Celtic Christianity's "religion-friendly" policy would not have been very controversial in the early Middle Ages; indeed, the Roman wing's mission practice often followed a similar policy. This is most memorably noted in the letter, which Bede has preserved for posterity, that Pope Gregory once sent to his missionaries at Canterbury.

> I have decided after long deliberation about the English people, namely that the idol temples of that race should by no means be destroyed, but only the idols in them. Take holy water and sprinkle it in these shrines, build altars and place relics in them. For if the shrines are well built, it is essential that they should be changed from the worship of devils to the service of the true God. When this people see

that their shrines are not destroyed they will be able to banish error from their hearts and be more ready to come to the places they are familiar with, but now recognizing and worshipping the true God. . . .[36]

Gregory also directed a missiological response to the Angle practice of slaughtering cattle as sacrifices to devils. "Do not let them sacrifice animals to the devil, but let them slaughter animals for their own food to the praise of God, and let them give thanks to the Giver of all things for His bountiful provision."[37]

So, the Roman wing of the Church would have had no serious problem with the Celtic movement's "religion-friendly" policy. We have seen, however, that the Roman wing of the Church had serious problems with the Celts' "culture-friendly" policy!

CHAPTER 7

The "Celtic" Future of the Christian Movement in the West

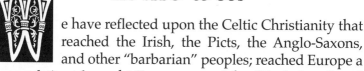e have reflected upon the Celtic Christianity that reached the Irish, the Picts, the Anglo-Saxons, and other "barbarian" peoples; reached Europe a second time; brought Europe out of the "Dark Ages" and "saved civilization"; and then was hammered into conformity by the Church's Roman wing. The story is a treasure within the total Christian story. The story, however, may not seem very "relevant" to Western churches in the twenty-first century. After all, the Celtic saga ended a thousand years ago, and it involved cultures and contexts very different from our age of cities, mass transportation, climate control, outer space, technology, and the Internet.

We have already addressed the "relevance" question at two points. Chapter 1 concluded with the suggestion that, as in Patrick's time, establishment Christian leaders still take a dim view of pastors and churches who befriend pagans, sinners, and lost people, and who make apostolic outreach the priority of a church. Establishment Christianity always expects its people, pastors, and bishops to care for, and fraternize with, church people.

Chapter 3 concluded by suggesting that, as in the case of the ancient Roman wing of the Church, denominations are still substantially in the hands of the less apostolic wing of the Church, which works overtime to gain and retain institutional control; which assumes it knows best; and which works persistently to impose Roman, European, or other culturally alien forms upon the more indigenous and growing movements within the denomination. This pathology is observed today, for example, in most of the denominations in the United States that were "imported from Europe."

Three additional suggestions should establish the relevance of the Celtic Christian story to much of what Western Christianity faces in the twenty-first century.

First, a host of New Barbarians substantially populate the Western world once again; indeed, they are all around us. Many of them are "secular"; that is, they have never been substantially influenced by the Christian religion; they have no Christian memory and no church to "return" to.[1] Many have never acquired a "church etiquette" (they would not know when to stand, or where to find Second Corinthians, or what to say to the pastor after the service), and they are not "civilized" or "refined" enough to fit and feel comfortable in the church down the street. Often, they are thought to lack "class." They may have unshined shoes or body odor or grease under their finger nails; in conversation, they might split an infinitive or utter an expletive. Many New Barbarians are addicted, and their lives are at least sometimes out of control around some substance, such as alcohol or cocaine, or some process, such as sex or gambling. Many Western cities appear, at least at times, to be taken over by the New Barbarians.

Second, these populations are increasingly similar to the populations that the movements of Patrick, Columba, and Aidan reached as the New Barbarians become increasingly postmodern. For over two centuries, the ideology of the Enlightenment shaped the climate of "Modernity" that profoundly shaped people's consciousness in the West. It scripted people to believe that they were essentially good and rational creatures; that they could build morality and society on reason alone; that science and education would deliver humanity from its remaining problems; that progress was "inevitable"; and that the universe functions like a machine—a closed system leaving no need for the supernatural and little room for spirituality.[2]

As the Enlightenment has faded, postmodern people are increasingly suspicious of people and institutions that claim Authority, and they are increasingly dubious of Ultimate Explanations. They are rediscovering their intuition, and they own and trust their feelings more. They take in the world through what they see, touch, and experience— not just through what they hear—and they explore spirituality and the supernatural.

The grounds of their identities are shifting. Prior to the Enlightenment, according to Martyn Atkins of England's Cliff College, people said "I belong, therefore I am." Under the Enlightenment's influence, people said "I think, therefore I am." Postmodern people now seem to be saying "I feel, therefore I am," or "I shop, therefore I am," or "I look good, therefore I am," or "I disobey, therefore I am," or "I doubt, therefore I am," or "I am, so what?" We also observe the "retribalism" of much of the West—as peer groups, subcultures, and ethnic groups produce an "I belong, therefore I am" source of identity once again.

Third, most churches assume (though this is seldom verbalized) that the postmodern New Barbarians are unreachable, because they are not "civilized" enough to become "real" Christians. Remarkably, most churches assume this in a time when the New Barbarians are often the most receptive people in our communities; many are searching "in all the wrong places" for the kind of life they yearn for. The typical church ignores two populations, year after year: the people who aren't "refined" enough to feel comfortable with us, and the people who are too "out of control" for us to feel comfortable with them! Several years ago, while consulting with a church, I did some laundry at the local laundromat and visited with eight people. Seven were unchurched; six had never been involved in any church; five would be interested, however, if a church was interested in them. I took their names and addresses to the church leader group and heard this response: "The people who frequent that laundromat aren't even nice."

So we can see enough parallels between the Celtic era and ours to understand the growing interest in Celtic Christianity. A renaissance in Celtic music, Celtic art, Celtic dance, Celtic love of nature, and Celtic spirituality is already under way. Sometimes, though, it is difficult to discern whether people are consciously plugging into Celtic Christianity or simply latching onto some of its themes without regard to their probable Celtic source.[3]

For example, eighteenth-century Methodism grew remarkably among England's working poor people who did not fit into the refined Church of England culture, whom Establishment Christianity largely ignored. John Wesley went to great lengths, through observation, interviews, and correspondence, to understand England's unchurched populations. Methodism, like Celtic Christianity before it, took root and became contagious almost everywhere in the open air. Wesley's movement practiced the ministry of hospitality and welcomed seekers into the fellowship of Methodist class meetings, and even into membership in Methodist societies, before they believed or had experienced anything. Most of them "caught" the faith from the fellowship. Methodism was a lay movement, which saw itself as an alternative community, which practiced the ministry of conversation, and which contextualized the message and addressed "middle" as well as ultimate issues. Methodist leaders were aware of the influence of *ethos* and *pathos,* and identifying with the target population in communicating the message. Wesley traveled to communities with an entourage, which ministered as a team to a community, usually with the goal to plant a Methodist society or to start new classes within a society. Methodism formed its people in ways reminiscent of the Celtic fivefold approach. Methodism engaged people's imaginations through Charles Wesley's poetry and the folk arts of the people. Early Methodism employed an alternative architecture in which people felt comfortable, which was conducive to fellowship and to sensing the imminence of the Triune God. Early Methodism adopted the people's kind of music, and many people sang their way into faith. Like the movement spawned by Patrick, Wesley's movement believed it had recovered the original apostolic mission to pre-Christian populations. Despite these (and other) similarities, and despite the fact that Wesley had read Bede's *Ecclesiastical History of the English People,* we cannot demonstrate that John Wesley was consciously appropriating themes from ancient Celtic Christianity. For the last thousand years, many Celtic ways have detached from their roots and freely circulated among the options that Christian leaders sometimes choose.

In the twentieth century, a number of academic fields have validated what the Celtic Christian leaders knew intuitively or from experience. The Celtic understanding that you help people find faith and The Way by bringing them into Christian community, and into the ministry of conversation, has been strongly validated in the field of the Sociology of Knowledge. Peter Berger's *The Social Construction of Reality*[4] features three major insights that especially validate the Celtic way: (1) A person's view of Reality is largely shaped, and maintained, within the community into which one has been *socialized.* (2) In a pluralistic society, the possibility of conversion, that is, changing the way one perceives essential Reality, is opened up through *conversations* with people who live with a contrasting view of

Reality, and (3) one adopts and internalizes the new world-view through *resocialization* into a community sharing that new worldview.

Once upon a time, only intuitive geniuses like Patrick and William Carey could make serious sense of other "cultures," but the insights and categories of Cultural Anthropology have equipped almost anyone, with time and effort, to understand another culture. A *culture* is defined as the learned pattern of beliefs, attitudes, values, customs, and products shared by a people. A culture is sometimes explained, metaphorically, as "the software of the mind" that has been "programmed" into a given people's shared consciousness through their enculturation.

Culture exists at different levels. There are "macrocultures"—like the Anglo, Arabic, Far Eastern, and Sub-Saharan African macrocultures, with multiple cultures within each (such as English, Palestinian, Korean, and Masai cultures). Some cultural anthropologists estimate that there are fourteen macrocultures on earth, and about thirty thousand peoples—each with its own name, culture, and language or dialect. Furthermore, most people live within one or more specific subcultures—such as the "Appalachian" subculture, or the "Baby Boomer" generational subculture, or the "horse racing" culture, or the "fitness" culture, or the "Culture of Addiction"—which extend across cultures and even across macrocultures.

People with addictions are among the most obvious, and least understood, New Barbarians in the West today. Secular society glibly labels such people as "drunks," "potheads," or "losers," and it is oblivious to the fact that no one chooses to become addicted and ignorant of the physical origins of addiction and the psychological, spiritual, and cultural forces behind addiction. Church people glibly explain addiction as "Sin"; then, as they assume that the power of Sin is greater than "the One who is in us," they shun, withdraw from, or even excommunicate people hijacked by addiction. Meanwhile, the academic study of addiction, in fields like genetics, psychology and cultural anthropology, has experienced enormous progress in understanding addiction.

Scholars now tell us that "an addiction is any substance or process that has taken over our lives and over which we are powerless."[5] One may become addicted to a "substance"—such as alcohol, drugs, nicotine, or even food. One may become addicted to a "process"—such as gambling, sex, relationships, or even religion. Whatever the specific addiction, the addictive personalities become more self-centered; they lose touch with their feelings; and they experience ethical deterioration and, in time, spiritual bankruptcy. The addiction takes over their lives incrementally, from use to misuse to abuse to addiction.[6] Geneticists tell us that some people, perhaps one in eight, are born with a genetic predisposition toward addiction.

We have advanced in our understanding of the psychology of addiction. We know that "denial" is the fundamental defense mechanism of addiction; addicts deny what is obvious to everyone else in their lives. When confronted, addictive personalities deny, minimize, or rationalize their problem, or they live with the illusion that they are "in control." They become liars in their relations with others, and with themselves; their memories become distorted and, like a tornado in the living room, they trigger chaos in the lives of the people who love them.

William L. White's *Pathways from the Culture of Addiction to the Culture of Recovery*[7] has demonstrated the astonishing complexity of addiction by showing that the addictive personality is sucked into a "tribe" or a "social world" that values, introduces, reinforces, and celebrates drug abuse and even shapes people over time into a different identity. For instance, the addiction tribe's new members acquire a new *language* and conversation themes, while losing the capacity to talk about their feelings. They enter a new world of *symbols*—paraphernalia, logos, specific clothing or jewelry, and "articles associated with hustling behavior such as beepers."[8] Addiction becomes involved with *institutions*, places (like the "saloon" in towns of the old West) associated with abuse, and with daily *rituals* that trigger abuse, such as after meals, or between activities, or more elaborate rituals like a needle-sharing ritual. The culture of addiction develops or uses *music,* like the rap music that legitimizes rage and glorifies cocaine use; that reaches repetitively into the addict's right brain to confirm the culture's beliefs and values, to make the drug lifestyle seem normal, and to trigger craving. The new recruit is gradually introduced to a local tribal *history* which is

passed on through stories and folktales. Most of these stories, which serve as a primary vehicle to transmit values, revolve around significant tribal events and personalities. "Hustling tales" become a way of transmitting knowledge and techniques to neophytes about various cons. Descriptions of heroes depicted in these tales become a way of shaping desired personality attributes of cultural members. "Copping tales" are used to teach neophytes the skills and dangers involved in procuring drugs. "Getting-off tales" convey a whole body of folklore and folk medicine on how to use and reduce risks associated with use. "Enemy tales" reinforce cultural paranoia and teach neophytes how to cope with cultural enemies, e.g., undercover agents, snitches, nonsmokers, supervisors, dealers who peddle "garbage," "shrinks," and "crazies."[9]

White describes some twenty different *roles* the tribal members enact to support and expand the culture of addiction. For example, the "dealer" provides drugs of choice for the members. The "high priest" champions the culture's values and drug use and targets possible new converts. The "storyteller" is the culture's oral historian. The "medicine man" has folk remedies for hangovers, overdoses, and infections. The "jailhouse lawyer" helps members cope with law enforcement agencies and treatment professionals. The other roles, like the "hustler," the "ambassador," the "celebrity addict," the "crazies," and the "profiteers" reveal the remarkably sophisticated culture that undergirds the addictive lifestyle.

White reports that, in time, involvement with the drug and with the drug culture changes a person's identity and religious orientation. While before drug use, some persons were religious, some ignored religion, and some were emotionally rejecting their religious roots, such differences disappear as addiction takes over. Addiction does not make atheists or agnostics.

> Addiction, until the latest stages, renders questions of God and religion insignificant. . . . Addiction is so consuming there simply is no energy available to raise religious questions, let alone ponder answers. Addiction becomes one's religion, drugs become one's God, and rituals of use become rites of worship.[10]

Because the total drug experience is so social, and consuming, and transformative, disengaging a person from the culture of addiction is often more difficult than disengaging the person from the drug. Indeed, membership and involvement in a "culture of recovery" is usually necessary for a person's liberation from the twin powers of the drug and the drug culture.

Some of the same categories which enabled us to describe the culture of addiction also serve for describing the culture of recovery. Bill White contends that changing one's *language* profoundly aids recovery.[11] Recovery involves shedding the conversation themes, jargon, profanity, hustling tales, and other features of "addictspeak," and acquiring conversation themes, language, and perspectives that help one to make sense of one's experience and to move into recovery and a renewed identity. Often, for example, the recovering addict will drop the nickname or alias of his or her drug culture experience and select another name. Likewise, people in recovery need to shed the *symbols,* daily *rituals, music,* and role models that fuel the addictive lifestyle (like converts from primal religions who burn their fetishes when converting to Christianity), and replace them with symbols, daily rituals, music, and role models that focus and empower recovery. One needs to say goodbye to the old *institutions,* that is, the "slippery places," and hang out at healthy, drug-free havens. Recovery involves acquiring a new oral *history* and a larger Story within which to understand one's life, and a new wisdom to guide one's life.

The culture of recovery exists and extends through people who play some twenty-one different roles. For example, the "high priest" is a person in recovery who skillfully and passionately articulates recovery principles to new members and to the outside world. The "elders" serve as role models for the life of sobriety and serenity. The "storyteller" is the culture's oral historian who teaches recovery values and wisdom through narrative; the "comedian" teaches and heals through humor. The "medicine man" is a folk healer. The "mentor" supports and guides people early in recovery.[12]

For most people, White says, recovery involves religious experience. Addictive people need to reconnect with their spirituality and with God and experience "rebirth"— defined as breakthrough in self-perception, decision to change, empowerment for new life, and the reconstruction of personal values.[13] For most people, all of this takes place within a recovery community.

A generation of addiction research has strongly validated the Celtic Christian awareness that we need to *understand* a "barbarian" population to reach and serve them, and the Celtic confidence that we can understand them and reach them. Bill White's "culture of recovery" also validates the Celtic Christian emphasis upon the role of community experience in people finding truth, life, and a new identity, and the role of daily rituals in reinforcing that identity. Increasing numbers of churches are liberating people from the culture of addiction by bringing them into an intentional Christian recovery community. Indeed, the "Twelve Step Movement" is this generation's underground awakening.

The power of Christian recovery communities is best observed in people. I have interviewed many people who experience deliverance from addiction's mysterious power through community experience and religious experience. An athlete in Southern California, in the 1970s, was featured in several movies until Hollywood passed him by. He experienced depression and he self-medicated with booze, which led to alcoholism and a bed in an intensive care unit. The Holy Spirit visited him in the hospital and gave him the power to walk out of the hospital and away from alcohol. Since I knew that a single religious experience, by itself, might not liberate someone for life, I inquired, "What community helps you stay in recovery?" He replied, "My church is my recovery community!" His story is exceptional only in the sequence of events. Most people get into the recovery community first, and then experience the power of God.

Increasing numbers of churches are becoming "recovery communities" or "Twelve Step churches." Meredith Whitaker was a church and community worker among Native American Indians in eastern Oklahoma when, in 1990, she was asked to lead services each Sunday for the struggling Canterbury Chapel United Methodist Church in

Vian, Oklahoma. For eighteen months, Meri Whitaker preached to two people (who ran off the occasional visitors!). Whitaker observed that many people in the community who were being helped in Alcoholics Anonymous groups needed to know more about God than the "Serenity Prayer," and they had nowhere to go to church.

Whitaker persuaded half of the (two) regular attendees to turn Canterbury Chapel into a Twelve Step church. They got the word out to the AA community, and twenty-seven came on the first Sunday. Whitaker indigenized the service to fit the AA culture; they begin with Reinhold Neibuhr's famous "Serenity Prayer":

> God, grant me the serenity to accept the things I cannot change, courage to change the things I can, and wisdom to know the difference.

Meri Whitaker often engages recovery issues in her sermons, and features what the people need to know about God beyond the "Serenity Prayer." They close by joining hands and praying together the Lord's Prayer. The church has a norm against coming to church "dressed up"; casual attire is expected, and Whitaker usually models the "casualization of Christianity" by leading the service wearing jeans.

In six and a half years, Canterbury Chapel Church has received about one hundred new members; most are in recovery and most had never gone to church before. Their average attendance in recent years, about sixty, was "standing room only" until they moved into a new two hundred-seat sanctuary in 1999, and changed their name to Serenity United Methodist Church.

Meri Whitaker observes that most church people are like Jonah; they assume that the "Ninevites" do not deserve God's love. Serenity Church, however, wants the people who wouldn't "fit" in most churches and, she reports, if someone cusses in church, "nobody gets bent out of shape!" As Whitaker interprets Serenity church's mission to other churches, she recalls the Sunday that a motorcycle gang of eight first visited the church. Before the service closed, one biker asked to say something: "I've been in prison for fifteen years. Damn, I didn't think I'd ever go to church, and I sure as hell didn't think I'd ever find a church that would have me. But I really need this." Whitaker pauses to let the biker's words sink in, and then says: "For those of you who are more concerned that I cussed in your church today than you are that there are people out there who think the church won't have them, I'm here to tell you—your priorities are all messed up."

The Serenity Church story illustrates the first of two types of opportunities that many churches face. Some churches serve communities where many people are already in Twelve-step recovery groups but need a church. In most communities, however, there are far more people needing recovery than there are recovery groups with leaders-in-recovery to serve them; in these cases, churches are starting, and multiplying, recovery groups as explicit ministries of the church.

Indeed, some Christian movements are pioneering very intensive recovery communities. For instance, New Horizons Ministries organizes recovery communities in Marion, Indiana, as well as in Ontario, Canada, and the Dominican Republic. New Horizons specializes in ministry to "out of control" teenagers with attention deficit disorder (ADD), or attention deficit hyperactive disorder (ADHD), or opposition defiance disorder, or addictive traits, or a pattern of self-destructive behaviors, whom parents and schools can no longer manage. New Horizons' community experiences involve structure, discipline, worship, scripture study, prayer, group experiences, journaling, counseling, labor projects, and physical activities in a natural wilderness setting. Tim Blossom, New Horizons' director, reports that students especially grow from the camaraderie they experience from helping each other, and from their service with poor people or with self-destructive children. The process takes months, but many teens find a new identity and a new life through such community experience. Tim Blossom reports that New Horizons, which began in 1971, was the pioneer in such ministry; today there are over five hundred such ministries in the United States.

The second half of the twentieth century experienced a widespread renewal of many other features of Celtic Christianity. Ian Bradley observes that some of the most influential Christian writers of the twentieth century, like John Baillie, Pierre Tielhard de Chardin, and Thomas Merton were drawing from a distinctively Celtic theological vision.[14] Celtic Spirituality now has many public leaders. I am told that Trinity College in Dublin, and the universities of Wales, Aberdeen, St. Andrews, Glasgow, Edinburgh, Durham, and Cambridge offer one or more degree programs in Celtic studies, though not exclusively in Christian Celtic studies.

In 1938, George McLeod rediscovered several Celtic Christian themes. He led the movement that restored the medieval abbey at Iona, Columba's ancient headquarters, and he launched the Iona Community as a force for church renewal and justice, prayer and healing, mission and evangelization.[15] Following McLeod's death, the Iona Community has dropped his interest in evangelization, and has redefined "mission" around causes like peace, justice, ecology, urban ministry, Gay and Lesbian causes, and "interfaith dialogue"—though I could find no records of the Iona Community actually participating in inter-faith dialogues. Iona is an inspiring place to visit, and it has a useful library, but I met no one on the staff who knew much about Celtic

Christianity or who sympathized with Celtic evangelical mission.

The Holy Island of Lindisfarne is moving in the opposite direction. David Adam, the rector of Holy Island, is the most prolific writer of devotional literature in the Celtic tradition. Ray Simpson now leads the Retreat Center at Lindisfarne and heads The Society of Aidan and Hilda— with a growing membership in Britain and beyond. Kate Tristram retired early as professor of church history at the University of Durham to head Marygate House at Lindisfarne, where she built a significant Celtic library. She may be the most articulate interpreter of Celtic Christian history.

Some Christian movements today, such as Revelation Church in the south of England, are consciously informed by a Celtic Christian vision. Revelation's leaders know that most postmodern people experience "belonging before believing," so they welcome the full involvement of seekers. Their goal is to plant churches so indigenous to each people group "that its expression will emerge from within their culture, in their language, styles and flavours, yet still embodying the counter-cultural values of the gospel."[16] Revelation churches involve their people in soul-friendships, small groups, lay ministries, the ministry of witness, and in cross cultural mission. They feature ministries for deaf people, addictive people, and people with disabilities. Revelation Church is discovering ways to communicate through visual symbols and the creative arts. The movement's leaders report that

> At times, within the context of our worship meetings, we have encouraged artists to come and draw what they feel is happening as the church worships together. We have also had sculptors and even potters working to one side of the meeting. Sometimes, in the process of the worship the artists are encouraged to interpret what it is they are portraying. At other times the work is left to stand in its own

right and people are invited to go and view it at the end and ask the Holy Spirit to speak to them.[17]

The Jesus Movement in Australia is also consciously Celtic in its roots and vision. The movement began around 1970, under the leadership of John Smith, as an outbreak of indigenous evangelistic and prophetic activity in Irish pubs, coffee shops, arts communities, folk music communities, hippie communities, and in debates on race and justice on university campuses. The movement evolved into an apostolic order in cooperation with several Australian denominations. The Australian Jesus Movement targeted people in (and beyond) the fringes of establishment society, such as bikers, hippies, naturalists, addictive people, alienated young people, "apocalyptic" people expecting the end of the world, and the "wandering seekers" who were experimenting with Eastern religions like Zen. Smith reports that the movement wanted "anyone who felt marginalized and alienated from the established culture, in one way or another." Occasionally, whole communities—such as the Garden Island Creek settlement in Tasmania—turned to Christ.

Smith would organize an itinerant team of a dozen to thirty or more people to engage a community for some days. Team members let their hair grow, traveled on motorcycles and, when appropriate, wore hippie shirts or leather jackets. Many team members were etched with Celtic Christian tattoos, which, Smith recalls, "stimulated questions everywhere!" After evening services, groups infiltrated bars and taverns to befriend, converse with, and invite people. If a team was reaching out in their own city, as many as one hundred people would fan out and engage pubs, art centers, and other locations where people converse. When on the road, they usually ministered with, and at the invitation of, the churches already in the community, with the goal of starting new groups and ministries for, say, men, or youth, or addicts. Where it was impossible to assimilate converts and active seekers into existing churches, the movement would start a new "St. Martin's Community Church."

St. Martin's Community Churches are experiments in indigenous Australian Christianity, especially for Irish immigrant populations in Australia, and are based on a perceptive analysis of the Irish cultural personality. John Smith observes that "the Irish know how to celebrate—with minimum resources and with minimum reasons (in the world's terms) to celebrate." One might almost guess, Smith muses, that the Irish are genetically encoded to be celebratory personalities. Furthermore, the Irish celebrate more or less the same, "whether in the pub, or the church, or the wake! They enjoy a joke on the deceased! And they enjoy a joke in church." Irish Christians, Smith says, see the Kingdom of God in part "as a party—where the doors are thrown open like an Irish pub to anyone who would come in." So Smith believes that church should feel something like an Irish pub—festive, music, participatory—with everyone welcome. "No one is going to check your credentials. Leave your attitude at the door, come in, find your place, and feel free to express your gift."

Though each St. Martin's church is somewhat different from the others, the first one, in Melbourne, is illustrative. The walls are of mud brick—in the Aussie "Outback Bush" tradition. The vertical support is provided by thick planks hewn from Australian gum trees. The sanctuary features two open fireplaces to suggest the church is a "house" of God. Soup is cooking in the large pot behind the podium, which will provide the communal meal that concludes the service. There is no baptistery; the movement baptizes converts in the nearby river—as a public event and an opportunity to publicly declare the gospel. The church was built largely by volunteers; a team of women made all the mud bricks. Some volunteers were seekers. The man who cut the gum tree planks was a seeker and, Smith recalls, "we saw him growing like a plant in the sun."

St. Martin's worship is, most of all, unrestrained uninhibited celebration, more or less "in the tradition of an Irish pub," Smith says. The services are long, by usual standards, and many of their people have short attention spans; six or eight schizophrenic people may be attending a service! Consequently, people are often entering and exiting the service, or getting up and walking over for coffee. The spirit of "unpredictability" hangs in the air!

Services feature clear and relevant biblical preaching which faces both the ultimate issues and the daily issues. Services encourage emotional self-expression and "the full expression of one's soul." Services feature storytelling, because Smith believes that "story engages deeply the Irish spirit—and all human spirits." The church's staple music is reminiscent of the Irish ballad, though they also include some ancient Christian music, and ancient and contemporary Celtic music, and music from other Christian traditions and cultures.

St. Martin's church encourages the full expression of the Christian imagination, and often features indigenous art, much of it postmodern (sometimes extreme), serving Christian themes. Wall hangings are often featured around the sanctuary, and perhaps a cross surrounded with barbed wire at the front. Once the leaders invited, and displayed, a hundred art pieces on the crucifixion. One featured a slaughtered lamb; another showed the dying man's genitalia—which, of course, reflected what crucifixion looked like and, therefore, one source of the public shame of crucifixion.

Some liturgies, especially during Advent and Lent, are rooted in very ancient traditions, but St. Martin's worship is more noteworthy for its spontaneity, and its openness and inclusiveness. For example, pedophiles are welcomed in the church, and are "accompanied" when they visit a restroom or a children's area. Each service is planned but, Smith recalls, "we will put the plan aside if it's necessary, for a redemptive moment." Once a man walked into a service with a can of beer and cursing. The service changed pace, welcomed him, drew him in, and today he is a "regular."

John Smith, like the ancient Celtic apostles, believes that affirmation and paradox, understanding and mystery, are all important in theology. He believes that some Truth is better expressed metaphorically and artistically than through theological propositions. He believes that we should "do church" in ways that are "ancient and liturgical, and also postmodern, spontaneous, and a bit profane." He believes that "sensuality and spirituality should be friends." In outreach, Smith reflects on the movement's adoption of hippie shirts, tattoos, etc., but comments that "you can't ape it or 'go native.' Your heart has to be in it, and really identifying with the people so much that you have common cause with the indigenous people," as in their love for nature, or their quest for justice. "They became our people. We joined in common cause with them." He especially believes in involving seekers in the community's fellowship and celebration. "Often," he reports, "we didn't know when evangelism ended and mutual celebration began."

Some Christian movements, such as the Alpha course from Holy Trinity Church in the Brompton section of London, may be *un*consciously informed by a Celtic Christian vision. The Alpha course served, for over a decade, as Holy Trinity's introduction to Christianity for seekers who want to "sniff around," "kick the tires," check out Christianity, and try it on for size. In the early 1990s, the church's leaders introduced other church leaders to the course and its growth has been remarkable—from 5 registered courses in 1992, to 10,500 in 1998—in 72 countries.

A seeker attends an Alpha Course for most of a season—one session a week for ten weeks, climaxed by a weekend retreat covering the last four sessions. The seeker discovers that she or he is an honored "guest" of a church that loves the ministry of hospitality. The seeker's experience, each session, begins with fellowship around a meal, followed by a welcome, a time of celebrative worship, a talk,[18] refreshments, and then a conversation time in a small group of eight to twelve people.

Alpha's leaders observe that, through the Alpha experience, seekers are partly socialized into Christian belief, and the small group experience is indispensable in this socialization process. A group's leader functions essentially as a host and conversation facilitator—rather than a speaker or teacher, and the seekers are treated like guests—rather than auditors or pupils. Within several weeks, the group leader has developed a pastoral care relationship with group members—encouraging people, praying for people, praying with people, inviting (without pressure) response to the Holy Spirit. Each week, group members ask their questions, and express their ideas and feelings, and discuss Christianity's possibilities for their lives. Frequently the group bonds and continues meeting as a group long after the Alpha course is completed. Most of Holy Trinity Church's new groups emerge from the Alpha courses, and most of the church's new leaders experience their initial development as group leaders; indeed, new converts often lead a group in the very next Alpha course.

The curriculum's theology is patently Trinitarian; the presentations are filled with humor, analogies, and other expressions from imagination to imagination, and from heart to heart. People experience the last four sessions, on the Holy Spirit, in a weekend retreat in a natural setting—because people are more likely to experience the Holy Spirit in nature.

The Alpha movement has raised up staff and laity to reach many New Barbarians for Alpha experiences. For instance, Bob Byrne lived a life of addiction, crime, and violence before a Christian woman explained the "fish" symbol on her lapel, invited him to follow Christ and to learn how through an Alpha course. Today, he is a theology graduate, an Anglican priest in Kent, and he leads Alpha courses for people who "society says are no good."

> I see people from all walks of life who don't know God and I know that is the most precious thing that they could possibly find.
>
> I like working with people nobody else wants to work with—people with drug problems, people who society says are no good. I do a lot of work in schools.
>
> My favorite kids are always the worst kids, because everyone else says they can't do anything with them. They are right: they can't, but God can.
>
> That's why I love Alpha so much. The beautiful thing about Alpha is that it digs and builds a foundation.[19]

A more recent issue of *Alpha News* reports Alpha courses in about one hundred prisons across the United Kingdom, and announces courses to be offered in all the prisons in Texas. One story features a former male model in the fashion industry, who experienced God's grace, made sense of the experience from an Alpha course at Holy Trinity, Brompton, and is now involved in volunteer ministry with AIDS families. Another story features a young man set free from drugs, and the drug culture, through his Alpha community experience. Still another story features a middle-aged man who experienced recovery from alcohol addiction in a Twelve Step program a decade ago, but still experienced "a great big hole inside of me." The Holy Spirit filled that hole during the final weekend retreat of an Alpha course.

Although there are many parallels between ancient Celtic Christianity and the contemporary Alpha course, the pastors responsible for the course for the last eight years—Sandy Millar and Nicky Gumbel—report no conscious appropriation of any models or insights from Celtic Christianity. It is possible that the original developer of the Alpha course, no longer on Holy Trinity's staff, was drawing on the Celtic Christian tradition. It is also possible that Holy Trinity, like increasing numbers of churches, has picked up some pieces of the Celtic way of doing church without conscious regard to their historic source.

Some of the Celtic Christian movement's achievements might not seem very achievable today—such as the way that their monastic communities created a center for community in the midst of "rural sprawl." We find today, however, many cases of "urban sprawl," and one of the secrets of the American "mega-church" has been its capacity to create a center for community in the midst of urban sprawl. If you flew over our section of metropolitan Lexington, Kentucky, for instance, you would detect no obvious pattern, plan, or center for community in this metropolitan region; you would see only a random patchwork of housing estates, subdivisions, horse farms, shops, etc.

Southland Christian Church, in our region, has become a mega-church averaging more than six thousand in attendance that provides a place for community in the midst of urban sprawl. In this region of the city, if you attend a concert or a play; if your teenager attends a private high school or is in a youth group; if you give blood or vote for a jailer or a president; if you play softball or your kid is a boy scout or plays soccer; if you do aerobics or attend a support group or study conversational Spanish; if you need an appliance or a piece of furniture or some vegetables—you probably come to Southland Christian Church.

The two most prominent Celtic approaches to evangelization—a monastic community welcoming seekers as guests and teams from the monastic community visiting settlements for weeks or months—might, at first blush, seem unavailable to churches today. None of us live in Celtic monastic communities, and it is not vocationally possible for most of us to relocate in teams for blocks of time. This is a case, however, in which the specific models cannot be replicated, but the principles can be applied in new relevant ways.

For instance, most local churches are called to create more intentional ministries of hospitality than they have yet considered. My colleague at Asbury, Dr. Christine Pohl, wrote her dissertation in Christian Ethics on the history of hospitality in the Christian tradition and has followed it with contemporary studies. She reports that her list of local churches who take hospitality seriously, and exercise it effectively, is extremely short. Some parachurch Christian communities, like the L'abri fellowships, have given it serious attention, but most local churches have not. The typical hospitality ritual in a church goes no deeper than inviting guest worshipers to sign the registration pad so someone from the church can visit them later, and maybe put a ribbon or a "guest" badge on their lapel in case someone wants to greet them.

I have learned, through interview research, that most pre-Christian visitors to a church feel anxious and vulnerable as they visit "foreign turf" but, often, something is going on in their life that they think a church might help with. Most church leaders, however, have never taken seriously the nonverbal communication that a visiting seeker is sending out. Their visit is the most misperceived signal in local churches today, and the church's most neglected opportunity. Often, following their visit, visitors feel ignored, or judged, or misunderstood, or unwanted, and they may conclude that God doesn't understand or want them either. What would a serious ministry of Christian Hospitality look like in your church today?

One type of church, the Cell Driven Church (or the Church of Small Groups)[20] appears to have effective ways to help seekers experience hospitality. For instance, New Hope Community Church in Portland, Oregon, has over five hundred lay-led small groups meeting each week. Each small group has a symbolic empty chair to fill every six months, so members regularly invite people to visit their group, and these groups are primed and skilled to include new people.

Some churches, like the Brooklyn Tabernacle, may schedule a five to ten minute period in the worship service when people spontaneously gather into groups of four or five, exchange names, share something that is going on in their lives, and pray for each other. Somewhat like the Celtic Christians of old, some churches deploy teams in ministry and witness to identifiable communities. New York City has thousands of communities of people who are found, more or less, in some specific location. The Brooklyn Tabernacle especially targets some of the New Barbarian populations who live or congregate in specific known places—homeless people, street people, addicted people, drug pushers, go-go dancers, prostitutes, male prostitutes, etc. In any season, the Brooklyn Tabernacle sends out several teams of people to several targeted locations—like a homeless shelter or a school bus parking area where male prostitutes sleep. The teams visit at the same time each week for a season or two. They engage in appropriate ministry, conversation, and prayer, and they invite people to a Brooklyn Tabernacle worship service.

Some churches and denominations use teams of people for church planting once again. Indeed, C. Peter Wagner reports that "Hiving off" is "the most common way of planting a daughter church."[21] In this model, a team of people from one church will join a church planter to reach a target community, in the same city or area, to plant a new church.

"Colonization" is a more radical expression of the same principle. This model requires that the people pull up roots, and find new jobs, homes, and schools in the target community.[22] My colleague at Asbury, Dr. Ron Crandall, tells me that some traditions—from Mennonites to Moravians—typically plant churches using a colonizing team. Dr. Charles Chaney reports that a Southern Baptist team of eleven laity from Amarillo, Texas, moved with Pastor Frank Radcliff to the Chicago area and started a church in Oak Park. Then they targeted the suburb of Woodridge, ten more people moved from Amarillo to join them, and within three years the Woodridge Church averaged over one thousand in attendance. In the following years, they planted additional churches for African Americans, Hispanics, and Filipinos.[23]

Some features of the ancient Celtic Christian movement are as relevant today as ever but, to my knowledge, are not currently implemented. For instance, the Celtic bishops were primarily evangelists rather than administrators; I know of no denomination with a Celtic job description for its bishops!

Some relevant Celtic Christian features are only occasionally expressed. For instance, I have interviewed people who have a "soul friend" without knowing what to call him or her. We occasionally observe a recovery of the Celtic love for nature in Christian communities, but more often outside of Christian communities. The proposal that we can reach people through their imaginations has been advanced in good books by Fred Craddock, Ralph Lewis, and Joe Harding, but not many Protestant churches have discovered the communicative power of poetry, story, or the visual arts. (Indeed, a majority of churches have not yet discovered that it is okay to make church interesting!)

Perhaps five to ten percent of America's churches are trying culturally relevant "contemporary" worship—with some adaptation to the pre-Christian population's style, language, aesthetics, and music, but few churches are even considering the kind of identification with people practiced by the Celtic Christian movement and reflected in this ancient Chinese poem:

> Go to the people.
> Live among them.
> Learn from them.
> Love them.
> Start with what they know.
> Build on what they have.[24]

Few churches have yet discovered what Celtic Christian leaders knew about Heibert's "excluded middle." Richard Mouw, president of Fuller Theological Seminary, contends that Western churches are called to help people understand

> God's day-to-day dealings with us in the midst of our practical uncertainties about, for example, our health, our financial resources, and our intimate relationships. When we fail to provide such an account, people—ordinary Christians—will turn to those elements of folk religion, such as new age.[25]

Mouw also contends that one reason for the success of some "televangelists" and mega-church pastors is their sensitivity to "excluded middle" questions and concerns![26]

Most churches still attempt to do evangelism (if they attempt it at all) by bringing in a professional or by reaching out as individuals; the Celtic way of team ministry and outreach is seldom tried, but much more promising. Most attempts at evangelism today still emphasize a one-way presentation, rather than the ministry of (two-way) conversation. Ray Simpson and Kate Tristram have adapted St.

Aidan's conversational approach to people to make it useful to any Christian reaching out. You engage people with a question like: "Are you a Christian?" or "Where do you stand with regard to the Christian faith?" If they say they are Christians you ask, "How could you be a better one?" If they say they are not you ask, "May I tell you something about it?"[27] and that begins a conversation.

The Celtic strategy of sending teams into "enemy territory" is almost never done today, but it is the greatest "apostolic adventure" available to most Christians. Indeed, in the great "silent retrenchment" of the last third of the twentieth century, most churches ceased doing much proactive outreach at all. In most cities, most of the *growing* churches are only responding to people who take the initiative to visit the church.

Finally, not many churches are yet following Christ to reach the receptive New Barbarians who are all around us. That is tragic because, deep down, most of these people want to experience God's forgiveness and acceptance; they would like a second chance and a new life. The Church has what they are looking for, but it is not offering it to them! Nevertheless, the Celtic Christian movement that won the West for a second time has shown us many ways for reaching the West for a third time—if we have the eyes to see, and if we can rediscover that lost people matter to God.

The supreme key to reaching the West again is the key that Patrick discovered—involuntarily but providentially. The gulf between church people and unchurched people is vast, but if we pay the price to understand them, we will usually know what to say and what to do; if they know and feel we understand them, by the tens of millions they will risk opening their hearts to the God who understands them.

Notes

1. The Gospel to the Irish

1. John T. McNeill, *The Celtic Churches: A History* A.D. *200 to 1200* (Chicago and London: The University of Chicago Press, 1974) p. 57.

2. From Liam de Paor's translation of "St. Patrick's Declaration," in Liam de Paor, *Saint Patrick's World: The Christian Culture of Ireland's Apostolic Age* (Notre Dame, Ind: University of Notre Dame Press, 1993) p. 99.

3. Ibid., p. 100.

4. Virtually no two scholars are able to agree on St. Patrick's key dates! R. P. C. Hanson presents the most comprehensive and judicious discussion that I have found. Essentially, Hanson calculates probable dates upon external evidence. For instance, Patrick's career presumably took place after the translation and dissemination of the version of the Bible that he uses, and before the conversion of the Franks—whom Patrick refers to as pagans in his "Letter to the Soldiers of Coroticus." By such reasoning, Hanson pegs Patrick's birth at around 390, his kidnapping in 406, his escape in 412, and his death around 460. Hanson estimates that Patrick went to Ireland as an apostolic bishop sometime between 425 and 435. (So, the traditional date for Patrick's entry into Ireland, 432, is as good as any other for the purposes of this study.) See R. P. C. Hanson, *Saint Patrick: His Origins and Career* (New York: Oxford University Press, 1968) pp. 171-88.

5. R. Pierce Beaver, "The History of Mission Strategy," in Ralph D. Winter and Steven C. Hawthorne, eds., *Perspectives on the World Christian Movement,* revised edition (Pasadena, Calif: William Carey Library, 1992) p. B-66.

6. Ibid., p. B-59.

7. Quoted in Beaver, "The History of Mission Strategy," p. B-62.

8. Ibid., p. B-65.

9. William Barclay, *The Master's Men* (Nashville: Abingdon Press, 1959). See also George G. Hunter, III, *How to Reach Secular People* (Abingdon, 1992) pp. 108-9.

10. Ralph Winter shows that, repeatedly, when the Roman Church refused to reach the "barbarians," the "barbarians" assaulted Rome. So, when the Church neglected outreach to the Goths, the Goths proceeded to overwhelm the Church and the "Christian" lands. Later, the neglected Vikings overwhelmed the churched lands again. Still later, the invasions of Muslim armies wreaked havoc in Christian lands. See Ralph D. Winter, "The Kingdom Strikes Back: The Ten Epochs of Redemptive History," in Ralph D. Winter and Steven C. Hawthorne, eds., *Perspectives on the World Christian Movement*, revised edition (Pasadena, Calif: William Carey Library, 1992) pp. B-3 to B-21.

11. See Nigel Pennick, *The Sacred World of the Celts* (New York: Harper-Collins, 1997) p. 10.

12. Brendan Lehane, *The Quest of Three Abbots: The Golden Age of Celtic Christianity* (New York: Viking Press, 1968) p. 8.

13. Thomas Cahill, *How the Irish Saved Civilization* (New York: Doubleday, 1995) p. 82. Nora Chadwick, in *The Celts*, revised edition (New York: Penguin Books, 1997) p. 138. Cahill explains that "In warfare, as in so many other aspects of Celtic life, there appear to have been superficial overtones, as is suggested by the *gaesatae* who fought naked in obedience to an archaic ritual tradition which apparently taught that nudity afforded some supernatural protection." That deeper meaning behind a nude army's appearance would not have been apparent to opposing armies!

14. See Nora Chadwick, *The Celts*, pp. 53, 139.

15. Ibid., pp. 154-55.

16. Patrick, in the years of his enslavement, would have discovered that the Celts had a far more sophisticated, and even "civilized," culture than their "public image" suggested. He became familiar with their art, music, poetry, and storytelling, and their laws, myths, and religion. Patrick knew that the Irish Celts were nonliterate *by choice*; they valued their strength as an oral, and rather intellectual, culture. Their lawyers and their "bards" (the storytellers who perpetuated their oral history) trained for twelve years; their druids trained for twenty years.

17. Ian Bradley, *Columba: Pilgrim and Penitent* (Glasgow: Wild Goose Publications, 1996) p. 20.

18. Liam de Paor, *Saint Patrick's World*, p. 23.

19. See Brendan Lehane, *The Quest of Three Abbots*, chapter 2.

20. Ibid., p. 42.

21. I found four ancient sources most useful—St. Patrick's "Declaration" and his "Letter Against the Soldiers of Coroticus," Muirchu's "Life of St. Patrick," and Tirechan's seventh-century collection of local traditions about Patrick's mission. All of these sources, and others, are now

in excellent English translation and in one volume—Liam de Paor's *Saint Patrick's World,* cited above.

22. This reflects the company of people that accompanied Patrick to Selc in Tirechan's collection of local traditions about Patrick's mission (see *Saint Patrick's World,* p. 166). On another occasion, Patrick's entourage consisted of "a crowd of priests, deacons, exorcists, porters and lectors, as well as boys whom he ordained" (p. 155).

23. Louis Gougaud, who wrote a comprehensive pioneering text on Celtic Christianity in the 1930s, tells us that "We find Patrick everywhere setting himself first of all to convert the great." One reason, Gouddard says, for focusing on the king was that the king owned all the property, so the king had to give the land needed for a church. See Louis Gougaud, *Christianity in Celtic Lands: A History of the Churches of the Celts, Their Origin, Their Development, Influence and Mutual Relations* (London: Sheed and Ward, 1932) pp. 38-39.

24. "Bishop Tirechan's Account of St. Patrick's Journey," in *Saint Patrick's World,* pp. 163-65, seems to represent one such public conversation as typical of Patrick's approach.

25. We do not know if the Christian band would have offered the eucharist to seekers, but I would not be astonished to learn that they did. Much later, John Wesley and eighteenth-century Methodism were to view the sacrament as a "converting ordinance" and welcome seekers to the Lord's Supper.

26. "Bishop Tirechan's Account of St. Patrick's Journey," in *Saint Patrick's World,* 163.

27. James Bulloch, *The Life of the Celtic Church* (Edinburgh: The Saint Andrew Press, 1963) p. 49.

28. We think that these provisional settlements seldom exceeded three hundred people. If tribes averaged three thousand people, then a tribe would be dispersed in, say, a dozen settlements in the same region.

29. In *Saint Patrick's World,* p. 129.

30. *Christianity in Celtic Lands,* pp. 44-45. A few scholars are less impressed with Patrick and his alleged achievements. The most deconstructionist, and hostile, is E. A. Thompson, *Who Was St. Patrick?* (Rochester, N.Y.: The Boydell Press, 1985). Thompson criticizes (pp. 150-51) what he views as Patrick's "narrow conception of the aims of his mission. He aimed to convert the pagans, to bring them to the point of baptism, and, having baptized them, to move on to deal with persons who were still pagan. He might even leave new converts for his clergy to baptize and exhort, while he himself hurried on elsewhere. His aim, in fact, seems to have been to 'convert' the maximum number of pagans. It almost amounts to a counting of heads. Two or three times he tells us

that the number of his converts amounted to 'thousands.' Sometimes it would seem that it was numbers alone which counted, not the results of conversion, not the effect on the lives of the converted. Having converted one group (we might think), he rushes on to the next."

Thompson believes that Patrick should have spent his priority time on worthier causes, like ransoming captives, rather than converting people from their religion to Christianity. Thompson paints Patrick as a modern "Lone Ranger" Elmer Gantry evangelist, and seems oblivious to Patrick's "team" approach to settlements, the role of cross-cultural analysis and witness, the time they spent with a people, and a dozen other factors.

Thompson appears to have no first-hand experience with any Christian movement, nor with any other culture than his own, nor with any other model of evangelization than some twentieth century revival model that he dislikes. His trashing of Patrick is an "inexpensive shot" from an academic ivory tower. Thompson reveals his Enlightenment bias in one of his few "positive" comments about Patrick: "He never claims to have perpetrated a miracle" (p. 154).

Remarkably, Thompson also claims that Patrick "left no model to future generations. He had no successors in the sense that no one learned from him: no one launched missions similar to his outside other frontiers in imitation of him" (p. 157). This book's perspective contrasts with Thompson's by 180 degrees. There were hosts of successors who reached the rest of Ireland, and Scotland, and much of England, and much of Europe, by doing more or less what he did.

31. Thomas Cahill, *How the Irish Saved Civilization*, p. 110.
32. From "St. Patrick's Declaration" in *Saint Patrick's World*, pp. 103-4.

2. A New Kind of Community, A New Kind of Life

1. Gilbert Marcus, "Rooted in the Tradition," in *Christian History*, Issue 60, Vol. XVIL, No. 4, p. 20.
2. Liam de Paor, *Saint Patrick's World: The Christian Culture of Ireland's Apostolic Age* (Notre Dame: University of Notre Dame Press, 1993) p. 95.
3. James Bulloch, in *The Life of the Celtic Church* (Edinburgh: The Saint Andrews Press, 1963) p. 49, believes Patrick began planting monastic communities very early in his Irish mission.
4. For such background insights, see *Saint Patrick's World*, p. 23.
5. Philip Sheldrake, in *Living Between Worlds: Place and Journey in Celtic Spirituality* (Boston: Cowley Publications, 1996), acknowledges the common assumption that Celtic monastic communities were usually located "in wild and isolated places" (p. 22), but he demonstrates that

the location was usually selected for access, not for seclusion. Indeed, he contends, "Nearly all the major sites that grew into important monasteries are in fact on major travel routes or at least, in terms of ancient human geography, in relatively accessible places" (p. 28).

6. Brigid in Ireland and Hilda in England were the two most notable abbesses of large monastic communities.

7. John Finney, *Recovering the Past: Celtic and Roman Mission* (London: Darton, Longman & Todd, 1996) p. 50.

8. In time, some of the great European universities emerged from these monastic communities.

9. *The Book of Kells* (on exhibit at Trinity College, Dublin) and *The Lindisfarne Gospels* are the most famous examples of this unique Celtic Christian art called "illumination." The Bible was the *only* book upon which a monastic community's artists practiced the art of illumination, which indicates their reverence for the scriptures as God's unique revelation.

10. This picture of Celtic monastic communities is, necessarily, general. Brendan Lehane suggests (*The Quest of Three Abbots,* p. 17) that "Individual abbots made rules, which were sometimes adhered to and quite often not; some monasteries became lively centres of learning, some took on the duties of social service. There was no central authority, no unified aim, and the story of each community is different from that of others."

11. Sheldrake, *Living Between Worlds,* pp. 38-39.

12. Ibid., p. 44.

13. Paul G. Heibert, "The Flaw of the Excluded Middle," in *Missiology: An International Review* 10:1 (January 1982): 35-47. The article is reprinted more recently in Heibert's book *Anthropological Reflections on Missiological Issues* (Grand Rapids: Baker Books, 1994) pp. 189-201.

14. Paul G. Heibert, "The Flaw of the Excluded Middle," in *Anthropological Reflections on Missiological Issues,* p. 197.

15. Ibid.

16. I have oversimplified Heibert's theory. He also shows that people tend to view *each* of the three levels from either a "mechanical" or an "organic" perspective. But that level of complexity is beyond what I need for this study.

17. Alexander Carmichael, *Carmina Gadelica: Hymns and Incantations* (Edinburgh: Floris Books, 1992). Used by permission of Floris Books.

18. Ray Simpson, "Contemplative Prayer," chapter 4 in *Exploring Celtic Spirituality: Historic Roots for Our Future* (Hodder and Stoughton, 1995) pp. 51-56.

19. *Carmina Gadelica,* p. 93.

20. Ibid., p. 35.

21. Ibid., p. 299.

22. Ibid., p.217.

23. Ray Simpson, *Celtic Blessings for Everyday Life: Prayers for Every Occasion* (Hodder and Stoughton, 1998).

24. Ibid., p. 5. Copyright © 1998 by Ray Simpson. Reproduced by permission of Hodder and Stoughton Limited.

25. Louis Gougaud, *Christianity in Celtic Lands: A History of the Church of the Celts, Their Origin, Their Development, Influence, and Mutual Relations* (Dublin: Four Courts Press, 1932) p. 65.

3. To the Picts, the Anglo-Saxons, and Other "Barbarians"

1. The Irish Gaelic version of his name, which writers often use today, is Columcille.

2. Edward Sellner, *Wisdom of the Celtic Saints* (Notre Dame, Ind.: Ave Maria Press, 1993) p. 92.

3. Ian Bradley, *The Celtic Way* (London: Darton, Longman, and Todd, 1993) p. 21.

4. See *The Coming of Christianity to Anglo-Saxon England* (London: B. T. Batsford, 1972) pp. 26. See pp. 22-30 for Mayr-Harting's full discussion of Anglo-Saxon paganism.

5. John Finney, *Recovering the Past: Celtic and Roman Mission* (London: Darton, Longman, & Todd, 1996) p. 65.

6. Finney, *Recovering the Past,* p. 55.

7. See Book II of Bede, *The Ecclesiastical History of the English People* (Oxford and New York: Oxford University Press, 1994) for Bede's account of the ministry of Paulinus. Bede reports on the later ministry of Aidan in Book III.

8. *The Coming of Christianity to Anglo-Saxon England,* p. 29.

9. James Bulloch, in *The Life of the Celtic Church* (Edinburgh: The Saint Andrew Press, 1963) p. 64, judges that "Augustine's success was practically confined to the southeast corner of England. Bishops were appointed to the sees of Canterbury, Rochester, and London, but even these dioceses had to struggle for existence." While some writers are most interested in the movement of Aidan in reaching Northumbria (the largest of England's early medieval kingdoms), Bulloch estimates that "All England north of the Thames was indebted to the Celtic mission for its conversion" (p. 72).

10. For a recent, and comprehensive, analysis of the fall of Rome, see chapter I, "The End of the World: How Rome Fell—and Why" in Thomas Cahill, *How the Irish Saved Civilization* (New York: Doubleday, 1995).

11. Tomas O Fiaich, "Irish Monks on the Continent," in James P. Mackey, *An Introduction to Celtic Christianity* (Edinburgh: T&T Clark, 1989) p. 106.

12. Tomas O Fiaich, "Irish Monks on the Continent," p. 104.

13. Bede's account of the Synod of Whitby is featured primarily in Book III, chapter 25 of his *Ecclesiastical History of the English People,* though he discussed the issues focused in the synod in many places.

14. This history is discussed in Nigel Pinnick, *The Sacred World of the Celts* (New York: HarperCollins, 1997) pp. 94-95.

15. David J. Bosch, *Transforming Mission: Paradigm Shifts in Theology of Mission* (Maryknoll, N.Y.: Orbis Books, 1991) p. 294.

16. Ibid., p. 95. Bosch was referring to Catholic practice in the wake of the Enlightenment, but the principle predated the Enlightenment more than one thousand years.

17. Nora Chadwick, *The Celts* (New York: Penguin Books, 1997) p. 222.

18. D. H. Farmer, trans., Bede, "The Lives of the Abbots of Wearmouth and Jarrow," in *The Age of Bede* (London: Penguin Books, 1988) pp. 185-208.

19. Ibid., p. 186.

20. Ibid., p. 189.

21. Ibid., p. 190.

22. See Bede's *Ecclesiastical History of the English People,* Book IV, chapter 1.

23. In an endnote that purports to "explain" this sentence (p. 400), the editors of the Oxford edition of Bede's *Ecclesiastical History* offer the unlikely explanation that, by "Greek customs," Bede is "referring to the danger of theological errors, in particular the Monothelete, or "one-energy," doctrine . . . " This explanation is an unwarranted stretch, however, because Bede's allusions to heresies are usually quite explicit, and because the explanation is undermined by Bede's own explanation in his very next sentence: "So [Theodore] was ordained subdeacon, waiting for four months until his hair grew, in order that he might receive the tonsure in the shape of a crown; for he had received the tonsure of the holy apostle Paul, after the Eastern manner." Bede reveals, in those two sequential sentences, that he virtually equated Roman customs with "the true faith," or at least that the true faith is totally dependent upon Roman forms for its protection and communication.

24. See Lyle E. Schaller, "European or American?" in chapter 7 of *The Interventionist* (Nashville: Abingdon Press, 1997) pp. 91-104. Schaller shows that all but one of the denominations "imported from Europe" are declining, and all but one of the denominations "made in America" are growing! The two exceptions actually prove Schaller's point. The Southern Baptist Convention, the one denomination imported from Europe that is growing, has reinvented itself several times. The Chris-

tian Church (Disciples of Christ), the one denomination "made in America" that is declining, represents that wing of the Restoration movement that marched to a European drum.

25. Schaller, in *The Interventionist*, demonstrates another two dozen comparisons between culturally European ways of doing church and culturally American ways of doing church. Anyone who has studied churches in two or more European countries has observed that the old European ways of doing church are not demonstratively more effective in Europe today than in the USA today!

26. Gustav Niebuhr, "Christianity's Rapid Growth Giving Africans New Voice," in *The Lexington Herald Leader* (December 13, 1998).

4. The Celtic Christian Community in Formation and Mission

1. *Recovering the Past: Celtic and Roman Mission* (London: Darton, Longman & Todd, 1996) p. 67.

2. Attributed to an Egyptian abbot named Moses, quoted in Esther de Wall, *The Celtic Way of Prayer: The Recovery of the Religious Imagination* (London: Hodder and Stoughton, 1996) p. 87.

3. See de Wall, *The Celtic Way of Prayer*, pp. 117-22 for a fuller description of the Celtic "soul friend" tradition. See John O'Donohue, *Anam Cara: A Book of Celtic Wisdom* (Cliff Street Books, 1997) for powerful reflection from within the Irish Soul Friend tradition.

4. Small groups were prescribed in Rule #21 of The Benedictine Rule, as follows: "If the community is rather large, some brothers chosen for their good repute and holy life should be made deans. They will take care of their groups of ten, managing all affairs according to the commandments of God and the order of their abbot. The deans selected should be the kind of men with whom the abbot can confidently share the burdens of his office."

5. Esther de Wall, *The Celtic Way of Prayer: The Recovery of the Religious Imagination*.

6. Ibid., p. 38.

7. Ibid., p. 43.

8. This translation is published in Oliver Davies and Fiona Bowie, *Celtic Christian Spirituality: An Anthology of Medieval and Modern Sources* (London: SPCK, 1995) pp. 41-43.

9. Much of the approach which follows is delineated in "The Rule of St. Benedict." For a recent English translation of Benedict's Rule, and an excellent commentary, see Esther de Wall, *A Life-Giving Way: A Commentary on the Rule of St. Benedict* (London: Geoffrey Chapman, 1996). Father

Michael Rodgers, coauthor with Marcus Losack of *Glendalough: A Celtic Pilgrimage* (Harrisburg, Penn: Morehouse Publishing, 1996) informs me that the Celtic monastic communities so substantially influenced the Benedictine monasteries on the continent that, in the ministry of Hospitality, the published Benedictine Rule reflects the ministry pattern of the Celtic communities.

10. Rule 66 of the Benedictine Rule provides that "At the door of the monastery, place a sensible old man who knows how to take a message and deliver a reply, and whose age keeps him from roaming about. The porter will need a room near the entrance so that visitors will always find him there to answer them."

11. John Finney, *Recovering the Past: Celtic and Roman Mission.*

12. John Finney, *Finding Faith Today: How Does It Happen?* (British and Foreign Bible Society, 1992).

13. Ibid., pp. 46-47.

5. How Celtic Christianity Communicated the Gospel

1. George A. Kennedy's translation of Aristotle, *On Rhetoric* (New York: Oxford University Press, 1991) is now the most useful English translation, although Lane Cooper's translation—Aristotle, *The Rhetoric of Aristotle* (Paramus, N.J.: Prentice-Hall, 1960)—is still the most widely cited. Edward P. J. Corbett and Robert J. Connors *Classical Rhetoric for the Modern Student,* Fourth Edition (New York: Oxford University Press, 1999) is an outstanding secondary source for discovering the strategic wisdom of Aristotle and the whole rhetorical tradition within Western scholarship.

2. Kennedy, trans., *On Rhetoric,* p. 36.

3. Quoted in Lester Thonssen, A. Craig Baird, and Waldo W. Braden, *Speech Criticism,* Second Edition (New York: The Ronald Press Company, 1970) p. 445.

4. From "Bishop Tirechan's Account of St. Patrick's Journey," in *Saint Patrick's World,* p. 171.

5. "Muirchu's Life of St. Patrick," in *Saint Patrick's World,* 180-81.

6. See "Saint Patrick's Declaration" in *Saint Patrick's World,* p. 102.

7. Kennedy, trans., *On Rhetoric,* p. 38.

8. Wayne N. Thompson, *The Process of Persuasion: Principles and Readings* (New York: Harper & Row, 1975) p. 59. The third chapter of Thompson's classic text gives a cogent review of the (mid-1970s) state of the art in *ethos* research and includes excerpts from a number of primary sources.

9. Helmut Thielicke, *The Trouble with the Church : A Call for Renewal.* John W. Doberstein, ed. (New York: Harper & Row, 1965) pp. 1-11.

10. Kenneth Burke, *A Rhetoric of Motives* (Berkeley: University of California Press, 1969).

11. Søren Kierkegaard, *The Point of View,* trans. Walter Lowrie (London: Oxford University Press, 1939) p. 38. Kierkegaard also includes material on his "indirection" method in *Concluding Unscientific Postscript,* trans. David F. Swenson and Walter Lowrie (Princeton, N. J.: Princeton University Press, 1944), and *Kierkegaard's Attack Upon "Christendom,"* trans. Walter Lowrie (Princeton, N. J.: Princeton University Press, 1946), and *Stages on Life's Way,* trans. Walter Lowrie (Princeton, N. J.: Princeton University Press, 1945). See also Raymond E. Anderson's classic article "Kierkegaard's Theory of Communication," in *Speech Monographs,* 30 (March 1963).

12. William Warren Sweet, *Revivalism in America* (New York & Nashville: Abingdon Press, 1944), p. xii.

13. Thomas Cahill, *How the Irish Saved Civilization: The Untold Story of Ireland's Heroic Role from the Fall of Rome to the Rise of Medieval Europe* (New York: Doubleday, 1995) p. 109.

14. See *Saint Patrick's World,* pp. 109-13.

15. Thomas Cahill, *How the Irish Saved Civilization,* p. 113. A few writers have *not* believed that Patrick identified with the Irish. R.C.P. Hanson, for instance, asserts that Patrick "had no particular love for the Irish. . . . He knew the Irish language. He knew something of the Irish society, . . . But he had no sympathy with Irish culture as such." See Hanson's article "The Mission of Saint Patrick," in James P. Mackey, *An Introduction to Celtic Christianity* (Edinburgh: T&T Clark, 1989) pp. 36-37. Hanson bases that conclusion upon his interpretation of several statements by Patrick that can be interpreted in other ways, and Hanson's interpretation is not usually the most obvious. Hanson, plausibly, argues that Patrick "certainly had no respect whatever for the religion of the Irish," (p. 37), a statement that warrants four responses. First, no one becomes a missionary to a people whose religion he or she greatly admires! Second, many missionaries, in every age, have identified with the receptor population without championing their religion! Third, as we will see in chapter 6, Patrick found things in their religion that Christianity could build on. Fourth, if the Irish people had not experienced Patrick identifying with them, they would not have responded to his message as they did.

16. See *St. Patrick's World,* pp. 175-97.

17. "Muirchu's Life of St. Patrick," in *St. Patrick's World,* pp. 180-81.

18. Ibid., p. 187.

19. Ibid., pp. 184-85.

20. Adamnan of Iona, *Life of St. Columba,* trans. by Richard Sharpe (London: Penguin Books, 1995).

21. Ibid., p. 105.

22. Ibid., pp. 179-80.

23. Bede, *Ecclesiastical History,* Book III, ch. 3.

24. Bede, *The Ecclesiastical History of the English People,* translated by Bertram Colgrave (Oxford and New York: Oxford University Press, 1969) Book III, chapter 4.

25. Bede, *Ecclesiastical History,* Book III, chs. 5, 17.

26. Ibid., Book III, ch. 17.

27. Ibid., Book IV, ch. 27.

28. Ibid., Book IV, ch. 23.

29. Quoted in Thonssen, Baird, and Braden, *Speech Criticism,* p. 420.

30. Quoted in Thomas Cahill, *How the Irish Saved Civilization,* p. 6.

31. Thomas Cahill, *How the Irish Saved Civilization,* pp. 96-97.

32. Ibid., p. 126.

33. Ibid., p. 115.

34. George Campbell, *The Philosophy of Rhetoric* (Carbondale: Southern Illinois University Press, 1988).

35. This chart is adapted from Johnston McMaster, *The Future Returns: A Journey with Columba and Augustine of Canterbury* (The Corymeela Press, 1997) p. 41.

36. Ian Bradley, *The Celtic Way* (London: Darton, Longman & Todd, 1993) p. 84.

37. Quoted in John T. McNeill, *The Celtic Churches: A History A.D. 200 to 1200* (Chicago and London: The University of Chicago Press, 1974) p. 40.

38. Ian Bradley, *The Celtic Way,* p. 85.

39. Ibid., p. 96.

40. Ibid., p. 90.

41. Ibid., pp. 1-2.

42. Ibid., p. 86.

43. Thomas Cahill, *How the Irish Saved Civilization,* p. 115.

6. The Missionary Perspective of Celtic Christianity

1. Adamnan admits that Columba preached to the Picts through an interpreter. See his ancient *Life of St. Columba* (New York: Penguin Books, 1995) p. 179.

2. David J. Bosch, *Transforming Mission: Paradigm Shifts in Theology of Mission* (Maryknoll, N.Y.: Orbis Books, 1991) p. 447.

3. Bede, *The Ecclesiastical History of the English People* (Oxford University Press, 1994) pp. 114-15.

4. Nora Chadwick, *The Celts*, New Edition (New York: Penguin Books, 1997) p. 197.

5. Twice, in the Letter, Patrick refers to the Picts as "apostate." See "St. Patrick's Letter to the Soldiers of Coroticus," in Liam de Paor, *Saint Patrick's World* (Notre Dame, Ind: University of Notre Dame Press, 1993) pp. 109, 112.

6. "Letter to the Soldiers of Coroticus," in *Saint Patrick's World*, p. 112.

7. Louis Gougaud, *Christianity in Celtic Lands: A History of the Churches of the Celts, Their Origin, Their Development, Influence, and Mutual Relations* (London: Sheed and Ward, 1932, republished by Four Courts Press, 1992) pp. 26-27.

8. Quoted in W. Douglas Simpson, *Saint Ninian and the Origins of the Christian Church in Scotland* (Edinburgh: Oliver & Boyd, 1940) p. 91.

9. David J. Bosch, *Transforming Mission*, p. 294.

10. Brendan Lehane, *The Quest of Three Abbots: The Golden Age of Celtic Christianity* (New York: Viking Press, 1968) p. 39.

11. Ibid., pp. 40, 111.

12. From "Bishop Tirechan's Account of St. Patrick's Journey," in Liam de Paor, *Saint Patrick's World: The Christian Culture of Ireland's Apostolic Age* (Notre Dame, Ind: University of Notre Dame Press, 1993) pp. 163-64.

13. From Douglas Hyde's *Carmina Gadelica*. Quoted in Oliver Davies and Fiona Bowie, *Celtic Christian Spirituality: An Anthology of Medieval and Modern Sources* (London: SPCK, 1995) p. 140.

14. Thomas Cahill, *How the Irish Saved Civilization: The Untold Story of Ireland's Heroic Role from the Fall of Rome to the Rise of Medieval Europe* (New York: Doubleday, 1995) p. 138.

15. Ibid., p. 126.

16. This summarizes material in the fifth chapter of Cahill's *How the Irish Saved Civilization*, but no summary can do justice to Cahill's moving development of this theme.

17. Bede, *Ecclesiastical History*, Book II, chapter 9, p. 84.

18. Ibid., Book II, ch. 9, p. 85.

19. Ibid., Book II, ch. 14, p. 97.

20. David Adam, *Flame in My Heart: St. Aidan for Today* (London: SPCK, 1997) pp. 96-98.

21. In the twentieth century, for instance, the experience of mission in the two-thirds world has enabled many Christian leaders to recover a Christian perspective upon the supernatural, and evil forces, and Christ's role as *Christus Victor*, which were features of original Chris-

tianity—but forgotten in the period of the Enlightenment's greatest influence upon Western church thought.

22. From "Muirchu's Life of St. Patrick" in Liam de Paor, *Saint Patrick's World: The Christian Culture of Ireland's Apostolic Age* (University of Notre Dame Press, 1993) p. 192.

23. Michael Mitton, *Restoring the Woven Cord: Strands of Celtic Christianity for the Church Today* (London: Darton, Longman & Todd, 1995) p. 58.

24. Indeed, one source suggests that "The Romans showed little love for the natural world and appear to have viewed it, like Plato before them, as a prison in which the soul is trapped." Roger Ellis and Chris Seaton, *New Celts* (Eastbourne: Kingsway Publications, 1998) p. 45.

25. Ian Bradley, *The Celtic Way* (London: Darton, Longman & Todd, 1993) pp. 53-54. All of chapter 3 is devoted to the theme of "The Goodness of Nature."

26. Philip Sheldrake, in *Living Between Worlds: Place and Journey in Celtic Spirituality* (Boston: Cowley Publications, 1996) p. 76, writes that, for Columbanus, "The 'incarnation,' as it were, of God in nature is . . . significant in two ways. First, it indicates unequivocally the closeness of God to us. . . . Secondly, nature is like a second revelation, a 'book' to be 'read' alongside the scriptures as we seek to deepen our knowledge of who God is."

27. Ian Bradley, *The Celtic Way*, p. 52.

28. Ibid., pp. 59-60.

29. I have avoided discussion, in the text, of the "Pelagian" controversy. Pelagius was a British Celtic theologian whose name is given to the view of human nature that has prevailed, more or less, in British Christianity. Augustine once organized a council of bishops in Africa to declare Pelagius a heretic. Multiple motives may have driven this trial. Pelagius was a layman. He recognized, and mobilized, the minds of women. He was obese and some people, like Jerome, intensely disliked him. Most of his key writings, to which Augustine was reacting, have not survived. Pelagius appears to have affirmed free will and rejected Predestination, and he may have believed in the possibility of universal salvation.

While Pelagius's teachings undoubtedly influenced the Briton Celtic church, there are reasons to doubt any appreciable influence upon the Irish, Pict, and Anglo-Saxon churches. One can detect no influence from Pelagius in Patrick's writings. Furthermore, the Irish monks who copied manuscripts did not know his writings, or they did not prioritize their perpetuation. Nevertheless, Pelagius's theology was not a strong factor in Celtic Christianity's theological vision. Their instincts were probably

"Semi-Pelagian," but they may have had no systematic theology of human nature, at least until Columbanus.

30. There is widespread interest today in the ancient religion of the Druids, although we don't know much about it. The fact that the Druids would not express their religious lore in writing, relying entirely on a twenty-year process of teaching it *orally* to the next generation of Druidic leaders, severely limits our knowledge of what they believed. Of course, that has not stopped some writers from pontificating, but most of these writers appear to be seeing their own reflection in the Druid pool of water!

31. "Bishop Tirechan's Account of St. Patrick's Journey," in *Saint Patrick's World*, p. 169.

32. Michael Mitton, *Restoring the Woven Cord*, pp. 90-91.

33. Ibid., p. 88.

34. "St. Patrick's Declaration," in *Saint Patrick's World*, p. 98.

35. Derek Bryce, *Symbolism of the Celtic Cross* (Samuel Weiser, Inc., 1989) p. 11.

36. Bede, *The Ecclesiastical History of the English People*, Book I, ch. 30.

37. Ibid.

7. The "Celtic" Future of the Christian Movement in the West

1. For much more on the "secular people" theme, see George G. Hunter III, *How to Reach Secular People* (Nashville: Abingdon Press, 1992).

2. For a fuller explanation of the Enlightenment, Modernity, and Post-modernity, see George G. Hunter III, *Church for the Unchurched* (Nashville: Abingdon Press, 1996) chapter 1.

3. Indeed, many themes we rightly attach to Celtic Christianity—like imagination, or love of nature, or hospitality, or conversation with seekers—are not unique to the Celtic Christian movement.

4. Peter L. Berger and Thomas Luckman, *The Social Construction of Reality: A Treatise in the Sociology of Knowledge* (New York: Doubleday, 1966).

5. Anne Wilson Schaef and Diane Fassel, *The Addictive Organization* (Harper & Row, 1988) p. 57.

6. Dick Schaefer, *Choices and Consequences: What to Do When a Teenager Uses Alcohol/Drugs* (Medina, Minn: Johnson Institute, 1996) p. 34.

7. William L. White, *Pathways from the Culture of Addiction to the Culture of Recovery: A Travel Guide for Addiction Professionals*, Second Edition (Center City, Minn: Hazelden, 1996).

8. Ibid., p. 56.

9. Ibid., p. 59.

10. Ibid., p. 54.

11. Ibid., pp. 268-75.

12. Ibid., pp. 395-407.

13. Ibid., pp. 275-85.

14. Ian Bradley, *The Celtic Way* (London: Darton, Longman & Todd, 1993) chapter 6.

15. George McLeod interpreted his early vision for the modern Iona Community in *We Shall Rebuild: The Work of the Iona Community on Mainland and on Island* (The Iona Community Publishing Department, 1994). That book focuses on the nature of, and need for, conversion and the mission of the congregation in helping people experience it, as well as the ways the Church must count in "the marketplace" through political and economic involvement. McLeod's more mature reflections, on similar themes, are found in *Only One Way Left* (The Iona Community, 1956).

16. Roger Ellis and Chris Seaton, *New Celts* (Eastbourne: Kingsway Publications, 1998) p. 76.

17. Ibid., p. 158.

18. The substance of the 15 "talks" is featured in Nicky Gumbel, *Questions of Life* (Eastbourne: Kingsway Publications, 1995). Another book by Nicky Gumbel, *Searching Issues* (Eastbourne: Kingsway Publications, 1995), which is for small group leaders, addresses the seven questions seekers ask most often in Alpha's small groups. Americans who are interested in the Alpha course can dial 1-800-36-ALPHA for these and other books, the interpretive video, and other Alpha resources.

19. "Why I Love Alpha, by the ex-prisoner whose favorite young people are the ones 'society says are no good,'" in *Alpha News*, U.S. Edition, no. 1 (August-November, 1998), p. 8.

20. I describe these churches in George G. Hunter, III, *Church for the Unchurched* (Nashville: Abingdon Press, 1996). The book describes "Apostolic Congregations," and chapter 4 describes the role of small groups in the life of these churches.

21. C. Peter Wagner, *Church Planting for a Greater Harvest* (Ventura, Calif.: Regal Books, 1990) p. 60.

22. Ibid., p. 62.

23. Charles L. Chaney, *Church Planting at the End of the Twentieth Century* (Wheaton, Ill.: Tyndale House, 1982) pp. 67-73.

24. I am indebted to my anthropologist colleague, Dr. Darrell Whiteman, for this poem.

25. Richard J. Mouw, *Consulting the Faithful: What Christian Intellectuals Can Learn From Popular Religion* (Grand Rapids: William B. Eerdmans Publishing Company, 1994) p. 52.

26. Ibid., p. 55.

27. Simpson's version is found in Ray Simpson, *Exploring Celtic Spirituality* (London, Sydney, and Auckland: Hodder and Stoughton, 1995) p. 170. Tristram's version was given in a presentation within a seminar on "Celtic Models for Local Churches" at Holy Island Lindisfarne in October, 1998.

SELECTED BIBLIOGRAPHY
on Celtic Christianity

Adomnan of Iona, *Life of St. Columba*. Trans. Richard Sharpe. London: Penguin Books, 1995.

Bede. *The Ecclesiastical History of the English People*. Ed. Judith McClure and Roger Collins. Oxford and New York: Oxford University Press, 1994.

———. "Life of Cuthbert," in *The Age of Bede*, Revised Edition. London: Penguin Books Ltd., pp. 41-102.

———. "Lives of the Abbots of Wearmouth and Jarrow," in *The Age of Bede*, Revised Edition. London: Penguin Books, pp. 185-208.

Bradley, Ian. *The Celtic Way*. London: Darton, Longman and Todd Ltd., 1993.

———. *Columba: Pilgrim and Penitent*. Glasgow: Wild Goose Publications, 1996.

———. *Celtic Christianity: Making Myths and Chasing Dreams* New York: St. Martin's Press, 1999.

Bryce, Derek. *Symbolism of the Celtic Cross*. York Beach, Maine: Samuel Weiser, Inc. 1995.

Bulloch, James. *The Life of the Celtic Church*. Edinburgh: The Saint Andrew Press, 1963.

Cahill, Thomas. *How the Irish Saved Civilization: The Untold Story of Ireland's Heroic Role from the Fall of Rome to the Rise of Medieval Europe*. New York: Doubleday, 1995.

Carmichael, Alexander. *Carmina Gadelica: Hymns and Incantations*. Edinburgh: Floris Books, 1992.

Chadwick, Henry. *The Early Church*, Revised. London: Penguin Books, Ltd., 1993.

Chadwick, Nora. *The Celts*, New Edition. London: Penguin Books, Ltd., 1997.

———. *The Age of the Saints in the Early Celtic Church*. Cardiganshire, Wales: Llanerch Publishers, 1960.

Clancy, Thomas Owen and Gilbert Markus. *Iona: The Earliest Poetry of a Celtic Community*. Edinburgh University Press, 1995.

Dale, Douglas. *Light to the Isles: Missionary Theology in Celtic and Anglo-Saxon Britain*. Cambridge: The Lutterworth Press, 1997.

Davies, Oliver and Fiona Bowie. *Celtic Christian Spirituality: An Anthology of Medieval and Modern Sources*. London: SPCK, 1995.

De Paor, Liam. *Saint Patrick's World: The Christian Culture of Ireland's Apostolic Age*. Notre Dame, Ind.: University of Notre Dame Press, 1993.

De Waal, Esther. *The Celtic Way of Prayer: The Recovery of the Religious Imagination*. London, Sydney, and Auckland: Hodder & Stoughton, 1996.

————. *Celtic Light: A Tradition Rediscovered*. London: HarperCollins, 1997.

————. *A Life-Giving Way: A Commentary on the Rule of St. Benedict*. London: Geoffrey Chapman, 1995.

Duncan, Anthony. *The Elements of Celtic Christianity*. Rockport, Maine: Element Books, Inc., 1992.

Edwards, David L. *Christian England: Its Story to the Reformation*. Grand Rapids, Mich.: William B. Eerdmans Publishing Company, 1980.

Ellis, Roger and Chris Seaton. *New Celts*. Eastbourne: Kingsway Publications, 1998.

Fiaich, Tomas O. Irish Monks on the Continent, in James P. Mackey. *An Introduction to Celtic Christianity*. Edinburgh: T&T Clark, 1989, pp. 101-139.

Finney, John. *Recovering the Past: Celtic and Roman Mission*. London: Darton, Longman and Todd Ltd., 1996.

Gougaud, Louis. *Christianity in Celtic Lands: A History of the Churches of the Celts, Their Origin, Their Development, Influence and Mutual Relations*. London: Sheed & Ward, 1932. Reissued by Four Courts Press, 1992.

Hanson, R. P. C. *Saint Patrick: His Origins and Career*. New York and Oxford: Oxford University Press, 1968.

————. "The Mission of Saint Patrick," in James P. Mackey. *An Introduction to Celtic Christianity*. Edinburgh: T&T Clark, 1989, pp. 22-44.

Joyce, Timothy J. *Celtic Christianity: A Sacred Tradition, A Vision of Hope*. Maryknoll, N.Y.: Orbis Books, 1998.

Lehane, Brendan. *The Quest of Three Abbots: The Golden Age of Celtic Christianity*. New York, N.Y.: Viking Press, Inc., 1968.

Mackey, James P. *An Introduction to Celtic Christianity*. Edinburgh: T&T Clark, 1989.

————. "Introduction: Is There a Celtic Christianity?" in James P. Mackey. *An Introduction to Celtic Christianity*. Edinburgh: T&T Clark, 1989, pp. 1-21.

MacLeod, George. *We Shall Rebuild: The Work of the Iona Community on Mainland and on Island*. The Iona Community Publishing Department, 1944.

————. *Only One Way Left*. Glasgow-Iona-Edinburgh: The Iona Community, 1956.

McMaster, Johnston. *The Future Returns: A Journey with Columba and Augustine of Canterbury*. The Corrymeela Press, 1997.

McNeill, John T. *The Celtic Churches: A History A.D. 200 to 1200.* Chicago and London: The University Press, 1974.

Mayr-Harting, Henry. *The Coming of Christianity to Anglo-Saxon England.* London: B. T. Batsford, 1972.

Mitton, Michael. *Restoring the Woven Cord: Strands of Celtic Christianity for the Church Today.* London: Darton, Longman and Todd Ltd., 1995.

Murray, Patrick. *The Deer's Cry: A Treasury of Irish Verse.* Black Rock, County Dublin: Four Courts Press, 1986.

O'Donoghue, Noel Dermot. *Aristocracy of Soul: Patrick of Ireland.* London: Darton, Longman & Todd, 1987.

Pinnick, Nigel. *The Sacred World of the Celts.* London: HarperCollins Publishers, 1997.

Rodgers, Michael and Marcus Losack. *Glendalough: A Celtic Pilgrimage.* Harrisburg, Penn.: Morehouse Publishing, 1996.

Sellner, Edward C. *Wisdom of the Celtic Saints.* Notre Dame, Indiana: Ave Maria Press, 1993.

Sheldrake, Philip. *Living Between Worlds: Place and Journey in Celtic Spirituality.* Cambridge and Boston: Cowley Publications, 1996.

Simpson, Ray. *Exploring Celtic Spirituality: Historic Roots for Our Future.* London, Sydney, and Auckland: Hodder & Stoughton, 1995.

————, ed. *Celtic Blessings for Everyday Life: Prayers for Every Occasion.* London: Hodder & Stoughton, 1998.

Simpson, W. Douglas. *Saint Ninian and the Origins of the Christian Church in Scotland.* Edinburgh: Oliver & Boyd, 1940.

Taylor, Thomas. *The Life of St. Samson of Dol.* London: S.P.C.K., 1925.

Thompson, E. A. *Who Was Saint Patrick?* Rochester, N.Y.: The Boydell Press, 1985.

INDEX